For David, Katie and George

10 Publishing
a division of 10 of those.com

This book is so refreshing! Clare introduced me to real women. The wife who used all her wealth to promote the Gospel inspired me. The wife who undermined her husband's joy and work warned me. Before I read this book I worried that I would be condemned by the perfect lives of these wives. Instead, I found that they needed God's grace and forgiveness every day ... like me!

Liz Cox, Family Worker, St Giles' C of E Church, Derby

Reading Christian biographies can sometimes leave us feeling inadequate in comparison, but this book in contrast presents seven very real women complete with weaknesses, failures, and imperfections. Although they lived at a very different time and in a very different culture each encounter challenges us to consider our attitudes to our own circumstances today. This is a great introduction not only to these women who served God in the past but also to an important period in church history. It will be a wonderful resource for women's groups as it comes complete with bible studies at the end of each chapter.

Karen Soole, Chairwoman of the Northern Women's Convention

Fascinating, insightful, challenging — both men and women, young and old alike, will benefit from this terrific book on some of the great evangelical women of church history. It made me pray for more like them, in zeal and in godliness, and could be one of the instruments God uses to answer that very prayer.

Lee Gatiss, Director of Church Society and Adjunct Lecturer in Church History at Wales Evangelical School of Theology.

Old Wives' Tales

Clare Heath-Whyte

Old Wives' Tales
© 10Publishing 2013 Clare Heath-Whyte
(Reprinted twice)

Published by 10Publishing, a division of 10ofthose.com

9D Centurion Court, Farington, Leyland, PR25 3UQ
England

Email: info@10ofthose.com
Website: www.10ofthose.com

ISBN: 978-1-909611-12-2

Unless otherwise indicated, all Scripture quotations are
taken from the Holy Bible: New International Version.

Copyright © 1973, 1978, 1984 by International Bible
Society.

Designed by Diane Bainbridge

Printed and bound by CPI Group (UK) Ltd, Croydon,
England, CR0 4YY

With vivid and colourful detail, Clare Heath-Whyte records the stories of these women who would mostly be unheard of if it wasn't for their famous husbands, but whose lives have much to teach women today about living for and serving Jesus wholeheartedly. They are not all great examples to follow; Clare is honest about the weaknesses and failings of these women. But there are lessons to learn from each and the readers are challenged to consider whether similar attitudes or habits are hindering godliness and spiritual growth in their own lives. This book is hugely relevant and helpful. I thoroughly recommend it!

Carolyn Lacey, Woodgreen Evangelical Church, Worcester

I loved Clare Heath-Whyte's book about real women, striving to live faithfully for Christ in a culture that was hostile to the Christian message. These 18th Century women seem strangely familiar - they struggled in their relationships with others and with God. Their lives were by no means perfect and some of them were not even that interesting. The unbelieving world criticised them and held them up to ridicule. Clare's book shows us how God works in and through his people despite their failings and difficulties. A great book for personal encouragement or for reading with a group.

Amanda Robbie - Author and blogger

ACKNOWLEDGEMENTS

With grateful thanks to everyone who has helped this book along its way.

To all at the Proclamation Trust ministers' wives' conferences over the years who have given me the excuse to find out about the fascinating women mentioned in this book.

To Boo Meirion Jones, Denise Buchanan and Jonathan Carswell for encouraging me to write it all down.

To Katie, whose leaving the nest prompted me to do something new to fill the gap.

To Dorothy and Nick Jones, for freeing up my Mondays for writing.

To George, for giving me computer time and putting up with me, and the Old Wives, for the past six months.

To David and my parents for reading the manuscript and making encouraging comments, and to Vaughan for not only reading it, but also providing the foreword.

To David (again) – in the words of John Newton:

> *I can do more business in two days when you are at home than in three when you are abroad. For though I sit many an hour in my study without seeing you, yet to know that you are in or about the*

house, and that I can see you when I please, gives a sort of composure to my mind: ... Though my attention to you may me leave something undone which I ought to have done...

My comfort and my care,
My safety and my snare,
You have been and you are!

However, I have great reason to bless God that I ever saw you.

(John Newton, Olney, 4 May 1774)[1]

CONTENTS

FOREWORD

Despite the title of this book, please don't imagine that the author is old. She is in fact remarkably young — exactly the same age as me. That is not as much a coincidence as you might think, as she happens to be my twin. She entered the world a little before me, as she never tires of mentioning, and claims that those were the best ten minutes of her life.

She may not be old, but she is certainly a wife — and a mother. That explains why, even though she is far more able than me, she is a few years behind me in writing her first book. It combines all her passions — history, family and, above all, Christ and his gospel. I may be biased, but I really do think it's superb and I am sure you will too.

No one could doubt the huge contribution of women in the great Evangelical Revival in the eighteenth century, having read this book. The old saying 'The hand that rocks the cradle rules the world' is no doubt overstated, but the influence of these seven women was immense. Clare brings their characters vividly to life in ways that will both attract and, at times, repel. They lived in very different times from ours, but their examples, for good and ill, have much to teach us today.

It's certainly not only a book for women. Men should read it too. Not just to enjoy the stories, but to be inspired by how greatly women can enhance their life and ministry, cautioned about unwise marriage choices, and chastened by the marital failings of even the greatest preachers. The individuals who emerge are not plaster cast saints, but real human beings. If God can use them, with all their faults, why not us?

Vaughan Roberts

INTRODUCTION

Why would anyone bother to read about a load of women who lived more than two hundred years ago in a world very different from our own and in a rather obscure century? Surely the sixteenth century would be more interesting? It's familiar, it's fun – it's got Henry VIII and his six wives and Queen Elizabeth and the Spanish Armada. Or perhaps even the nineteenth century: Queen Victoria, railways, *Oliver Twist* and *A Christmas Carol*; Even the seventeenth century has Cavaliers and Roundheads, the plague and the Fire of London. The eighteenth century is generally seen as the boring bit in between, at least in Britain: the agricultural revolution and lots of dull kings called George.

The kings may have been a bit dull and/or mad and there are certainly more interesting things to study than the invention of the seed drill, but in terms of church history, the eighteenth century is one of the most exciting and important of all. The great nineteenth-century bishop J.C. Ryle said that at the start of the eighteenth century from 'a religious and moral point of view, England was sound asleep'.[1] By the start of the nineteenth century, it was very much awake. Evangelicals were becoming influential in all areas of life, from politics to education and business. Lives were changed as the gospel was preached and its implications for society were realized.

What had made the difference? The Evangelical Revival had made the difference – led by great men such as John and Charles Wesley and George Whitefield in Britain, Jonathan Edwards in America, and built on by the following generation of men such as John Newton.

But why bother with the women? Most of them were not exceptional. They were ordinary Christian women, trying to live for Christ in challenging times. If they had not been related to these great men we almost certainly would know nothing about them. But because they were, we do, and the way they served Jesus in their lives can encourage us as we seek to serve Him in ours. They are part of that 'great cloud of witnesses' of faithful believers from the past, whose lives can encourage us to 'run with perseverance the race marked out for us'.[2]

In many ways the challenges facing these women in the eighteenth century were very different from our own. There was no struggle to maintain a work-life balance – the concept of a career woman was a long way in the future. Education for women was rare, and from birth the likelihood was that they would be dependent on their father, husband or sons. For almost all married women, life consisted of childbearing, child-rearing and household chores – without any of the labour saving devices that we take for granted. It was a very tough life; no antibiotics or painkillers, and around 40 per cent of the population died in childhood. Grief and pain were everyday experiences. There were no pensions, NHS or benefits, and real poverty and hunger beckoned if the breadwinner was ill, grew old, died, or, in the case of Susanna Wesley's husband, Samuel, went to prison.

However, in some ways, although the details may have been very different, the difficulties of living a godly life in an ungodly world were similar to our own. Morality was something to be mocked. Drunkenness was rife, and although there were no cars, even in London, very few street lights, town centres on a Saturday night in the eighteenth century would in many ways seem familiar to us today. Hogarth's prints of *Gin Lane* show crowds of people guzzling cheap alcohol – it was said you could get drunk for a penny and dead drunk for tuppence. This situation had arisen as a direct result of government policy to support the distilling industry. Like today, profit trumped morality. It was a time when the slave trade was developing fast, and high-class prostitutes such as Kitty Fisher[3] enjoyed celebrity status, with the press printing every detail of their sexual adventures. Child prostitution was common, and after the restraint of the English republic under Cromwell, all the old vices were back with a vengeance – bear-baiting, cockfighting – whatever took your fancy. There were also the everyday temptations to conform rather than be transformed; to trust in self rather than Christ; to complain about, rather than be content with, the life God has given us. As now, it was not an easy time to be a godly woman.

The church did not provide much of a lead, either. Although Jane Austen wrote at the start of the nineteenth century, the Church of England she described was similar to that in the eighteenth century. Clergy, like Edward Ferrars in *Sense and Sensibility*, were often from wealthy families. 'The church' was a respectable occupation, leaving plenty of time for hunting and visiting friends. Any genuine Christian 'enthusiasm' was frowned upon. The Church of England seemed more concerned about conforming to society than challenging it. Nonconformist churches were not much better. Having sprung up in the much freer atmosphere during and after the Civil War, things had gone downhill. After the restoration of the monarchy and the introduction of the new prayer book in 1662, ministers who refused to use it were denied a licence, and nonconformist churches had become pernickety, dogmatic and inward-looking, with little concern for the lost.

Those women who tried, and often succeeded, in living a faithful Christlike life in that atmosphere can surely teach us something as we try to do the same more than two hundred years later.

Clare Heath-Whyte

Author's Note: There are names and places in this book where spelling appears as original.

CHAPTER ONE

Susanna Wesley

Godliness in an ungodly world

It would be great to be really godly, wouldn't it? It would be great to live wholeheartedly for Jesus, and to live to please Him. If only the world around us was less hostile; if only there were more opportunities to develop our gifts; if only our personal circumstances were easier; if only we were less busy – if only!

Susanna Wesley was a godly woman in a hostile world, with very few opportunities and difficult personal circumstances which meant she had no choice but to have a very busy life. She was the mother of Charles and John Wesley, the founders of Methodism. In the United States there are numerous churches, schools and family centres named after her. She is almost seen as the patron saint of the home schooling movement, and from some Internet sites you could get the impression that not only was she sinlessly perfect, but also that she herself was the prime mover behind the entire Evangelical Revival of the eighteenth century. But if she had not been the mother of famous men we almost certainly would not have heard of her.

Susanna was an exceptional woman, but like most women of her generation, and many in ours, her life was focused entirely around her family. She never held any position of influence in society or politics, and compared to the life of a woman in the twenty-first century she had few outlets for her many gifts. But it was the way that she lived that life that has led many to see her as a role model for Christian womanhood. She was not perfect, but she was determined to live for Christ in whatever circumstances she found herself . She is said to have explained, 'I am content to fill a little space if God be glorified.'

Susanna was born in 1669, at least a generation before the other women in this book. She was born at a difficult time, but also into personally difficult circumstances. Nowadays we may think of a family with any more than four children as being unusually large – but Susanna was born into a family that was unusually large even by seventeenth-century standards. When a family friend was asked how many children Samuel Annesley, Susanna's father, had, he replied, 'I believe it is two dozen, or a quarter of a hundred.' Susanna's brother-in-law, John Dunton commented, 'This reckoning of children by dozens is a singular circumstance; an honour to which few persons ever arrive.'[1]

Susanna was the youngest of *twenty-five* children. For many years there was little to live on, as her minister father had been thrown out of the Church of England in 1662, when he along with 2,000 others refused to abide by the new prayer book. By the time Susanna was born, the rules had been relaxed and the family had moved to London where Samuel started a meeting house in Little St Helen's Bishopsgate (now known as St Helen's Place). But money was always short and life was never easy.

Susanna did, nevertheless, have some advantages when she was growing up. Although large and poor, Susanna's family was loving and stable. Her father does seem to have been a very godly man who took the education of both his sons and daughters seriously. Susanna was very clever, and from a young age studied theology and French and possibly even Latin and Greek. For an intelligent child, her home was an exciting place to be. It was a meeting place for some famous thinkers of the day. Daniel Defoe, who wrote Robinson Crusoe, was a member of her father's congregation, and he and others would meet to discuss all the current theological and political ideas. She was clever, but she was also a very godly child. She determined when she was quite small never to spend more time in leisure than she did in personal devotion. She reminded her son Samuel of this in a letter: 'I will tell you what rule I observed in the same case when I was young, and too much addicted to childish diversions, which was this – never to spend more time in any matter of mere recreation in one day than I spent in private religious duties'[2] – a practice she kept to all her life. Imagine a modern-day child choosing to spend the same amount of time praying and reading the Bible as they did playing, watching TV and messing around on the computer!

She was not just godly, she was extraordinarily self-disciplined. This self-discipline was just one part of a very strong personality. Although her strength of character certainly helped her to go against the flow and live a godly life in an ungodly world, it also caused family friction. At the age of 13 she decided to join the Church of England, even though her father had suffered so much by leaving it. As you can imagine, it didn't go down well, although her father accepted her decision graciously. She later claimed that by the age of 13 she had understood and considered all the arguments for and against joining the established church.[3] Perhaps she had, but there may have been other less intellectual reasons. Her future husband, Samuel Wesley, was a frequent visitor at her father's church and also at their home. He was six years older, also from a nonconformist family, and at almost the same time had decided to 'change sides' and join the Church of England. They finally married when she was 20 and he was 26.

They both had equally strong and stubborn personalities and, although their marriage seems to have been a genuine love match, their life together was not always easy. Writing to John in 1725 when she had been married for thirty-seven years, she wrote 'tis an unhappiness almost peculiar to our Family, That your Father and I seldom think alike'.[4] On one infamous occasion, Susanna refused to say 'Amen' to Samuel's prayer for the well-being of William III, who Susanna did not believe was the legitimate king. Later her son John described what happened:

> *The year before King William died my father observed that my mother did not say Amen to the prayer for the king. She said she could not; for she did not believe that the Prince of Orange was a king. He vowed that he would never cohabit with her 'till she did. He then took his horse and rode away; nor did she hear anything of him for a twelve month. He then came back and lived with her as before.*[5]

Susanna didn't make matters easier by writing to those she knew would agree with her position. The Reverend George Hickes encouraged her to stand firm and told her to 'stick to God and your conscience which are your best friends'.[6] Susanna refused to back down and it was only after the family faced ruin when the rectory was burned down (for the first time!) that Samuel returned.

In that argument, Susanna's behaviour made the situation worse, but most of the difficulties she faced over her long life were not of her own making. She and Samuel struggled financially throughout their forty-six years together. Both came from relatively poor families, which meant that when Samuel entered the Anglican ministry they, unusually for the time, had very little financial support. In 1690 Samuel became the rector of the parish of South Ormsby in Lincolnshire. On a low income and with a new baby arriving every year, it was only Susanna's thrift that kept them afloat. Samuel was hopeless with money and believed that publishing his writings would help pay the bills. Although initially a few works went to print, his main project, a very long commentary on the book of Job, was never even finished.

Things got worse when the family moved to their new parish of Epworth, Lincolnshire. Samuel's politics and strict moral standards were not appreciated by his parishioners. One of the family's main sources of income was the flax that was grown on the glebe land, and they kept cows for milk and cheese. To show their dislike of the rector, parishioners burned the flax harvest and mutilated the udders of their cows, as well as chopping off the leg of one of their dogs. They were constantly harassed. One night a gang kept up a constant din outside the house by banging and shouting. The wet nurse caring for the youngest child was so tired that she rolled over and smothered the baby in her sleep. Emotionally, the persecution must have been devastating, and financially it was disastrous. The rectory was set on fire twice. The first time it had to be repaired. On top of all their other financial difficulties, this finally plunged the family into debt.

Outside his church, just after a baptism service, Samuel was arrested and sent to prison in Lincoln Castle for non payment of debt. He was there three months, leaving Susanna to cope alone with a large family in a hostile parish, with no money. The second time the rectory was burned down, the family was asleep inside and could easily have been killed. John, 6, was miraculously rescued at the last minute, leaving Susanna to conclude that he was destined for future greatness.

The loss of their home meant that all the children had to be farmed out to local families while a new house was built, so all of Susanna's careful and meticulous parenting was undermined. As if that wasn't enough, their new home was apparently haunted for several months by a poltergeist they called Jeffrey. The family seem to have been totally bemused by the banging and flying furniture. Samuel, who had been away when the haunting began, was unsurprisingly sceptical about the whole business, but was forced to change his mind when he experienced broken nights' sleep as domestic items flew about the bedroom. Whatever was going on suddenly stopped when the family decided the best course was to treat Jeffrey as a joke. The poltergeist never bothered them again.

Throughout these years, Susanna gave birth to nineteen children, only ten of whom survived infancy. She was also frequently ill, and from a young age suffered from rheumatism. She was often simultaneously pregnant, in pain, caring for small children and grieving for the loss of a child.

Today we cannot imagine coping with such hardship. In the West, we may find it challenging if we are not able to afford a foreign holiday or replace an ageing car. We feel we are justified in moaning if our lives do not turn out as we had hoped. We are used to the safety net the state provides when things go wrong, and even moderate suffering can cause people to turn away from God. Susanna did not just cope with her situation, she praised God for it and managed to work within it to glorify God. From prison her husband wrote: 'All this, thank God, does not in the least sink my wife's spirits. She bears it with the courage which becomes her, and which I expected from her.'[7] She used the gifts, personality and circumstances that God had given her to glorify Him.

How did she manage to do that? Above all, she had a godly perspective on her life which enabled her to praise God whatever she went through, as she viewed her sufferings in the light of eternity. She wrote realistically about her difficulties, 'I have enough to turn a stronger head than mine. And were it not that God supports me, and by His omnipotent goodness often totally suspends all sense of worldly things, I could not sustain the weight many days, perhaps hours' but then she continued, 'Upon the best observation I could ever make, I am induced to believe that it is much easier to be contented without riches than with them.'[8] Again, she wrote:

> I think myself highly obliged to adore and praise the unsearchable wisdom and boundless goodness of almighty God for this dispensation of His providence towards me. For I clearly discern there is more mercy in the disappointment of my hopes, than there would have been in permitting me to enjoy all that I had desired.[9]

She trusted in God's omnipotent goodness. She knew

that He was in control of every detail of her life and that every detail, however painful, was being used by Him for her good, as she grew to know Him better and trust Him more in preparation for meeting Him face to face. As she encountered yet another crisis she summed up her attitude: 'Courage then; think of Eternity.'

This attitude was developed over a lifetime of prayer and Bible-reading. Nothing would divert Susanna from praying. If there is one anecdote that people know about Susanna Wesley, it is that when she was in a kitchen full of children and she wanted to pray, she would put her apron over her head to show that she was not to be disturbed. She may certainly have done this for an emergency 'arrow prayer', but even with her large family she never wavered from her childhood pattern of never spending 'more time in any matter of mere recreation in one day than I spent in private religious duties'. Each day she spent at least two hours in prayer and Bible study. She considered prayer a real privilege.

If but some earthly prince or some person of eminent quality were certainly to visit you, or you were to visit him, would you not be careful to have your apparel and all about you decent, before you came into his presence? How much more should you take care to have your mind in order when you take upon yourself the honour to speak to the Sovereign Lord of the Universe.[10]

After the birth of her last child, Kezia or Kezzy, she found more time to study and to write. Once her older children had left home she wrote to them weekly, and often included theological reflections in her letters. She also wrote theological treatises on the Lord's Prayer and the Ten Commandments, and later a defence of her son John's ministry, which was anonymously published. Her writings show a woman of deep personal faith and wisdom, but some of her theology was pretty unorthodox. She prayed for, and even to, the dead. She was devoted to Christ and wrote at length in her letters about his work on the cross; however, she lacked assurance of forgiveness until shortly before her death. The epitaph that her son Charles wrote for her headstone implies that he thought that she had not been a true Christian until shortly before she died.

> ... *True daughter of affliction, she,*
> *Inured to pain and misery,*
> *Mourn'd a long night of griefs and fears,*
> *A legal night of seventy years.*
> *The Father then revealed His Son;*
> *Him in the broken bread made known;*
> *She knew and felt her sins forgiven,*
> *And found the earnest of her heaven ...*

Although she had, perhaps, focused on the pursuit of holiness, which could appear a bit legalistic, to call her long life 'a legal night of seventy years' seems harsh. The new Methodist movement's emphasis on 'enthusiasm' and emotion was at odds with the much more formal and intellectual approach of Susanna's generation. Through her writings we can see that she genuinely loved the Lord Jesus. Her love for Christ and her godly priorities influenced every aspect of her life. She was determined to do all she could to bring up her children to know and trust the Lord. Particularly after the disastrous second fire, in which John so nearly died, she rededicated herself to her children's education. In 1709 she wrote to her eldest son, Samuel, who was by that time away at school at Westminster, 'There is nothing I now desire to live for, but to do some small service to my children, that as I have brought 'em into the world, so that it might please God to make me (though unworthy) an instrument of doing good to their souls.'[11] Although, like her father, she valued education for both boys and girls, it was her children's souls that were her chief concern.

So often today, the ambitions of Christian parents for their children are startlingly similar to those of their non-Christian friends – a good education, successful career and happy relationship. We may say we value the Christian education of our children, but often our true priorities are exposed by the amount of time and money we spend on 'fulfilling our child's potential' compared to 'doing good to their souls'.

Susanna educated the children at home not out of principle, but from necessity. There was no money for education, but the three boys were able to go away to boarding school at age 11, this having been paid for by rich benefactors. The girls were entirely educated by their mother. She expected the same high standards of self-discipline in her children as she herself displayed. She developed a very strict set of moral and educational rules based on biblical principles by which the family lived. Sin and disobedience would be punished – but then mentioned no more. Good deeds should be commended. Each child's education started the day after their 6th birthday. After the birthday celebrations were over, work was to begin. Each child learned to read by working their way through the Bible, starting at Genesis.

Very unusually for the time, none of the girls were to focus on domestic duties until they had learned to read. Perhaps even more unusually, all of the children, boys as well as girls, were expected to help around the house. It does not seem that the children were naturally beautifully behaved, but their mother got the best out of them. One scholar has described the Wesley children as 'a cluster of bright, vehement, argumentative boys and girls, living by a clean and high code, and on the plainest fare; but drilled to soft tones, to pretty formal courtesies; with learning as an ideal, duty as an atmosphere and fear of God as law.[12]

Susanna always treated each of her many children as individuals. She spent an hour a week with each child to find out about their interests and spiritual state. As each child left home, she continued to put aside the same amount of time by writing them letters. She kept them in touch with all the family news. There is a fascinating letter to the eldest son, Samuel, describing all the personal details of the second fire, such as, 'We had no time to take our clothes, but ran all naked.'[13] Only a little later, although she was obviously still preoccupied by the devastation caused by the fire, she wrote to Samuel again. This time she was back to her usual self, focusing on his spiritual welfare, reminding him to 'Begin and end the day with him who is Alpha and Omega'. She also warned him to avoid the typical temptations facing a teenage boy.

If you indulge your unruly passions, if now you suffer yourself to love the world or anything in it, more than God, if you now neglect your private duties, your daily sacrifices of prayer and thanksgiving, or grow remiss or cold in their performance. If you now permit impurity, anger, hatred, malice or any kind of danger of intemperance to gain an ascendant over your mind, you are in danger of being eternally lost.[14]

Her letters to John after he left home covered many

tricky theological issues, and he often asked for her advice, even when he had become a celebrated religious leader.

Susanna's system for parenting and home education was thorough, godly and time-consuming – but did it work? Samuel, John and Charles all grew up to be moral and God-fearing men. John and Charles obviously went on to be the leaders of one of history's most dramatic revivals. However, they both said they were only converted in adulthood. As John wrote to a friend in 1738:

> *I feel what you say (though not enough), for I am under the same condemnation. I see that the whole law of God is holy, just, and good. I know every thought, every temper of my soul ought to bear God's image and superscription. But how am I fallen from the glory of God! I feel that 'I am sold under sin'. I know that I, too, deserve nothing but wrath, being full of all abominations, and having no good thing in me to atone for them or to remove the wrath of God.*

Soon after, John wrote in his journal:

> *In the evening I went very unwillingly to a society in Aldersgate Street, where one was reading Luther's preface to the Epistle to the Romans. About a*

quarter before nine, while he was describing the change which God works in the heart through faith in Christ, I felt my heart strangely warmed. I felt I did trust in Christ, Christ alone, for salvation, and an assurance was given me, that He had taken away my sins, even mine, and saved me from the law of sin and death.

The next morning, Wesley wrote: 'The moment I awaked "Jesus, Master" was in my heart and in my mouth.'[15] Their elder brother, Samuel, became a headmaster and pillar of the community, but was very antagonistic towards the 'enthusiastic' faith of his brothers and, later, his mother. Their seven sisters' lives were generally not very happy, but that was largely due to the lack of suitable and available husbands in rural Lincolnshire. Of the six that did marry, none had successful marriages. One died in childbirth a year after the wedding, one married a polygamist, three married violent drunks, and one faced financial ruin. Mehetabel (thankfully the family called her Hetty) ran off with a local lawyer who had no intention of marrying her. She returned home pregnant, and vowed to marry the first man who would have her. She was an educated, intelligent girl, but was married off to a local plumber, one of the already mentioned violent drunks.

From outward appearances, it may appear that Susanna's

rigorous educational system failed, but in very difficult circumstances Susanna did the best she could and was a good mother. She gave all her children, both boys and girls, a good moral and biblical education. She prayed for them and encouraged them until the day she died. Perhaps she did overemphasize the pursuit of holiness at the expense of grace, but in the religious context of her day she did her best to bring her children up to trust in Christ. Eventually, all but one did put their trust in Christ. It is a good reminder that there is no fail-safe method of parenting that will produce Christian children. As John realized, conversion is a work of God's grace, but Susanna played her part diligently and effectively.

Susanna was not just concerned for the spiritual welfare of her children, she also longed to see her husband's parishioners changed by Christ – and not just because their hostility had caused her so many problems. As the rector's wife, she was expected to be involved in visiting the poor and sick, but there were not many other opportunities for ministry. Her husband was a delegate to the Church of England's Convocation, the eighteenth century equivalent of General Synod, which required him to spend several months at a time in London.

While he was away, the temporary curate chose to preach, week by week, on the subject of debt avoidance.

Unsurprisingly, Susanna did not feel that this was of any great spiritual benefit to his congregation. On Sunday afternoons she started holding a small meetings for her family and servants, in which she read from Samuel's collection of sermons and led the gatherings in prayer. Soon the servants were bringing family and friends, some of whom had never attended church before. It was not long before the entire ground floor of the rectory was full to overflowing with up to two hundred people attending each week. The curate wrote, complaining, to Samuel, who wrote to his wife to tell her to stop. She replied:

> ... though the superior charge of the souls contained in the household lies upon you as the head of the family and as their minister, yet in your absence I cannot but look upon every soul you leave under my care as a talent committed to me under a trust by the great Lord of all the families of heaven and earth. And if I am unfaithful to Him or to you, in neglecting to improve these talents how shall I answer unto Him when He shall command me to render an account of my stewardship.[16]

Eventually, Samuel relented and allowed Susanna to continue with the meeting. The results were extraordinary. She wrote:

Besides the constant attendance on the public worship of God, our meeting has wonderfully conciliated the minds of this people towards us, so that we now live in the greatest amity imaginable; and what is still better, they are very much reformed in their behaviour on the Lord's day; and those who used to be playing in the streets, now come to hear a good sermon read, which is surely more acceptable to Almighty God.[17]

The parishioners, who had previously made the family's life miserable, were transformed. On Samuel's return the meetings stopped, but the effects lasted; there were no more mutilated cows or disrupted nights' sleep.

Not only was Susanna's life as a wife and mother difficult, but as a widow she faced an uncertain future. Samuel died in 1735, and Susanna had to leave the rectory. She was now entirely dependent on the generosity of her children. She moved five times in the space of four years, initially living with her unmarried daughter, Emilia. While she was there, John and Charles mentioned their plans for travelling across the Atlantic to Georgia on an evangelistic mission to the American Indians. She was recently widowed, destitute and in need of the support of her family. They both said they would only go if they had her heartfelt approval.

She replied, 'Had I twenty sons I should rejoice that they were all so employed, though I should never see them more.'[18] It was soon after they returned from what proved to be a disastrous missionary journey that they were converted.

After her stay with Emilia, she lived with her son Samuel, then with her daughter Martha (and her rather dubious husband), first in Salisbury and then in London, before finally settling with John at the Foundery, the new Methodist headquarters, in 1739, where she lived until her death in 1742. In those few years she had to cope with the deaths of both her eldest child, Samuel, and of her youngest, Kezzy.

Despite this grief, it seems that her last years were good ones. As she got more involved with the new Methodist congregation at the Foundery, she enjoyed Christian fellowship and encouragement. For once in her life, she was able to enjoy receiving rather than giving. As she heard good biblical preaching, her assurance of forgiveness and her enjoyment of the blessings she had in Christ increased. Shortly before she died she wrote, 'My dear saviour, art thou come to help me in my extremity at last?'[19] She died with her family around her, and her funeral, which John conducted, was attended by 'innumerable' members of her new church family.

In many ways, Susanna Wesley lived a 'little' life. She was, as many women still are, someone's daughter, someone's wife, and someone's mother. The circumstances and the time in which she lived to us seem almost unbearably hard. She had few of the opportunities or advantages that we enjoy in the twenty-first century, but she managed to live a life that glorified God. She was not perfect and she made mistakes, but she used her gifts, her situation and even her difficulties to grow closer to Christ herself, and to encourage others to do the same.

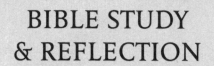

BIBLE STUDY & REFLECTION

Colossians 3:1 – 4:6

1. In what ways did Susanna's life live up to Paul's teaching here in

   - *her priorities and attitude to material things (3:1,2)*
   - *her attitude to her children's education (3:4–10)*
   - *teaching the parishioners (3:16)*
   - *her relationship with her husband (3:18)*
   - *her prayer life (4:2)*
   - *her attitude to criticism (4:5,6)?*

2. What challenges did Susanna face as she tried to live a godly life?

3. How do those challenges compare to the ones you face?

4. How can these verses and Susanna's life encourage and challenge us as we try to live godly lives in our particular circumstances?

CHAPTER TWO

Sally Wesley
Culture or Christ?

What influences us most in the way we live day to day? Are our decisions more likely to be based on the attitudes of the world around us, or by our desire to live for Christ whatever the cost? Perhaps when we began the Christian life we were 100 per cent committed, but as time goes by it is easy for priorities to shift. There's more pressure at work, the family demands more time, and maybe we become more concerned about worldly comfort and success than God's kingdom. In Sally Wesley, we can see that this is not just a twenty-first century issue.

Susanna Wesley was clearly an exceptional Christian woman. She stood out in the ungodly society in which she lived. She had remarkable gifts and, very unusually for a woman of her time, we can find out about her from her own words, as well as from those of her family and friends. We can only know Sally Wesley, Susanna's daughter-in-law, from a distance, largely through comments and letters of those who knew her. She was an ordinary Christian woman living in an extraordinary time, and married to an extraordinary man. In some ways she was admirable, and in some ways not; so we can be challenged by her mistakes as well as inspired by her successes.

Sally was the wife of Charles Wesley. John and Charles Wesley both made a pact that they would never marry. Although the stated reason was to free themselves for ministry, their sisters' unhappy marriages and their parents' less than perfect relationship must have affected their decision. Both of them did remain single until middle age, and then both married within a short time of each other. Charles, the younger of the two, married Sarah (Sally) Gwynne in April 1749, and the couple enjoyed a happy marriage for the next thirty-nine years – a major achievement in the Wesley family.

By this time, the religious make-up of Britain had begun to change. The constant preaching of the Wesley brothers and others up and down the country was having an impact as they travelled from town to town, speaking in whatever space was made available to them, in or out of doors. Charles had already written many of the hymns that we still sing today. *Hark the Herald Angels Sing* and *And Can It Be* had already been published along with hundreds more. John and Charles were famous men, adored by some and hated by others for their enthusiastic style and call for conversion and changed lives. The following extract from Charles' journal during a trip to Ireland in 1748, the year before his marriage, shows some of the excitements and dangers of the early years of the revival.

> *Mon. morning, February 8th, took horse for Tyril's-pass. We overtook a lad whistling one of our tunes. He was a constant hearer, though a Roman, and joined with us in several hymns which he had by heart. Near seven we got, half choked with the fog, to Mr. Force's. The town immediately took the alarm, and crowded in after us. I discoursed on, 'A certain man had two sons,' &c. These are the publicans that enter before the Pharisees. Never have I spoke to more hungry souls. They devoured every word. Some expressed their satisfaction in a way peculiar to them, and whistled for joy. Few such feasts have I had since I left England. It refreshed my body more than meat or drink.*

> *God has begun a great work here. The people of*

Tyril's-pass were wicked to a proverb; swearers, drunkards, Sabbath-breakers, thieves, &c., from time immemorial. But now the scene is entirely changed. Not an oath is heard, or a drunkard seen, among them. ... They are turned from darkness to light. Near one hundred are joined in Society, and following hard after the pardoning God.

Wed., February 10th. At eight I took horse for Athlone. We were seven in company, and rode mostly abreast. Some overtook us, running in great haste, and one horse-man, riding full speed. We suspected nothing, and rode on singing, till within half a mile of the town. Mr. Samuel Handy and Jonathan Healey happened to be foremost, three or four yards out of the line, though I had led the company till then. We were mounting a little hill, when three or four men appeared at the top, and bade us go back. We thought them in jest, till the stones flew. J. Healey was knocked off his horse with a stone, fell backward, and lay without sense or motion. Mr. Handy, setting spurs to his horse, charged through the enemy, and immediately turned upon them again. There were only five or six ruffians on the spot; but we saw many gathering to us from all sides.

I observed the man who had knocked down J. Healey striking him on the face with his club; cried to him to stop, which drew him upon me, and probably saved our brother's life, whom another blow might have dispatched. They had gathered against our coming great heaps of stones, one of which was sufficient to beat out our brains. How we escaped them, God only knows, and our guardian angels. I had no apprehension of their hurting me, even when one struck me on the back with a large stone, which took away my breath.[1]

———————————◆•◆•◆———————————

The early Methodist preachers were endlessly travelling. Those were the days before railways or even well-maintained roads. Coaches were uncomfortable and slow. John and Charles usually travelled on horseback for speed and economy, and stayed in whatever accommodation was available, however rough. There was no regular income, and violent attacks were common. Not surprisingly, John Wesley had assumed that this lifestyle was only suitable for single men.

Then Charles met Sally. It was love at first sight, and although apparently Charles had, a little earlier, begun to consider the idea of marriage in the abstract, it now became a real and attractive possibility. In many ways, Sally seemed very suitable. She came from a keen Methodist family. Her father, Marmaduke Gwynne, was a wealthy Welsh landowner and magistrate who had been converted under the preaching of the great Welsh evangelist Howell Harris in 1737. As a magistrate, having heard reports that Harris's preaching was a danger to both church and state, he prepared to arrest him when he arrived in his area. He told his wife, 'I'll hear the man myself before I commit him',[2] and so, with a copy of the Riot Act in his pocket, he joined the congregation, waiting to spot if any of Harris's words could be seen as seditious.

Harris was not arrested. Marmaduke Gwynne was so impressed by what he heard that he shook Harris by the hand, apologized for his suspicions, and invited him back to his home for supper. From then on, he used his influential position to protect the Methodist preachers from prosecution, and his home in Garth, near Builth Wells in mid Wales, was often visited by the Wesleys and others on their travels.

However, in some ways Charles and Sally were an unlikely couple. She was 21, he was nearly 40. She had been brought up in considerable luxury in a large house with twenty servants, a resident chaplain and room for at least fifteen guests. He had been brought up in relative poverty and, as an itinerant preacher, had little hope of keeping her in the manner to which she was accustomed.

After he had gained his brother John's approval for the match, and had his proposal accepted by Sally, Charles then had to persuade the Gwynnes that he was a suitable husband who could provide for their daughter. He enlisted the help of Sally's sister Becky, who spoke to her mother on Charles' behalf. He was relieved to hear that Mrs Gwynne stated that 'she would rather give her child to Mr Wesley than any other man in England'[3] The only problem was his lack of money. There then followed protracted negotiations. Mrs Gwynne wanted to be sure that Charles could guarantee that Sally would have at least £100 a year. To Charles that was a vast amount of money, but to Sally even living on £100 would mean a considerable drop in living standards. Eventually, John suggested using the income from Charles's musical publications to provide the income. This money would otherwise have been added to Methodist funds, and this alternative use of church assets was controversial. Later in their marriage, Sally's expectations and background were again to cause some resentment among the generally much poorer members of their congregations.

For now, though, with the financial settlement agreed, the wedding could go ahead. Hymns he wrote shortly before his marriage shows how much he was looking forward to a lifetime of fellowship, support and encouragement.

> *My gifts and comforts all, I know,*
> *From Thee alone descend;*
> *Thou only couldst on me bestow*

So true, and kind a friend.
Cast in one mould by art Divine
Our blended spirits agree,
And pair'd above our spirits join
In sacred harmony.

Let us both together rise,
To Thy glorious life restored,
Here regain our paradise,
Here prepare to meet our Lord.
Here enjoy the earnest given,
Travel hand in hand to heaven.[4]

The brothers travelled to Garth for the ceremony, but the journey from London took longer than expected as John agreed to preach along the way. As Charles wrote in his journal: 'I had wrote our friends notice, that I should be at Cardiff to-morrow, and on Tuesday or Wednesday at Garth. But I found my brother had appointed to preach in several till Friday; which I did not take kindly.'[5] Finally the wedding day arrived, as Charles noted in his journal: 'Sat., April 8th. "Sweet day! so cool, so calm, so bright, The bridal of the earth and sky." Not a cloud was to be seen from morning till night. I rose at four; spent three hours and an half in prayer, or singing, with my brother, with Sally, with Beck. And led MY SALLY to church.'[6]

He spent the next fortnight with his new wife (when he 'preached constantly'), and then set off on the road again. He obviously missed Sally, and with letters the only means of communication – and no efficient postal service – he really valued those he received. Three weeks after the wedding he noted in his journal, 'Fri., April 28th. Some letters from Garth brought life with them. I prayed and wept over the beloved writers.'[7]

When she married, Sally had promised that she would never hinder Charles in his travelling ministry, and also that she would not stop him being a vegetarian. She did her best to keep both promises. Initially, when possible, Sally travelled with Charles, despite the difficulties and dangers. This entry in Charles's journal the year after they got married gives a good impression of the everyday discomfort of travel in the eighteenth century:

1750 Wed., August 8th. It rained hard soon after we set out; but quickly gave over. We had a rough, dangerous passage at Frommelow. We dined at Cambridge inn, and had a trying journey, 'driven by the wind, and battered by the rain.' Sally was frightened with the thunder, which often forced us to trees and huts for shelter. Yet at seven, by the assistance of God, we entered our own house in peace.[8]

On one occasion, they narrowly escaped a highwayman on Hampstead Heath, and they were often greeted by hostile mobs ready to heckle and throw rotten vegetables to silence the preachers.

In temperament, Charles was much more emotional and sensitive than either his mother or his brother John, and he really appreciated having a loving wife to support him, both on the road and as a stable presence at home. He wrote frequently when she was unable to travel with him, both to show how much he missed her, and to her encourage her in her Christian life: 'My prayer for my dearest partner and myself is, that we may know Him, and the power of His resurrection. ... My heart is with you. I want you every day and hour. I should be with you always, or not at all; for no one can supply your place.'[9] Far from hindering her husband's ministry, Sally was determined to encourage and support him in it however she could. Only a couple of days after returning home from the 'rough, dangerous passage' and 'trying journey' we read, 'Fri., August 10th. Sally accompanied me in my visits to the sick.'[10]

Charles bought a small property in Bristol soon after they got married, which he said 'suited a stranger and pilgrim upon earth'.[11] It was very different from the home in which Sally had been brought up in, but she adapted well and used it as a place to show hospitality to other travelling preachers. Throughout her life, she also used her beautiful singing voice in Methodist chapels to encourage the believers. The Reverend Francis Fortescue wrote of her in his diary that Mrs Wesley, 'who is upwards of eighty years of age, sung, to our great astonishment, two of Handel's songs most delightfully – "He shall feed His flock," etc. and "If God be with us," etc.'[12]

However, she was not always seen as an asset to his ministry. John, in particular, criticized her for encouraging Charles to stop his itinerancy and settle down, first in Bristol and later in London. In fact, she does not seem to have put any pressure on him to stop travelling, but after a miscarriage in 1750, possibly brought on by a difficult journey, Sally gradually stayed at home more while her husband was preaching around the country. This certainly contributed to his decision to stop travelling too. Although he often tried to persuade her to join him he was rarely successful and, unlike most husbands of the time, he never forced her. In a letter of 1760 he wrote, 'The greatest earthly blessing I could obtain were a sight of you and your children; but I should not buy it too dear; if you came unwillingly. Therefore do as you find best or not at all. Your will I shall receive as the will of providence.'[13]

Although John was very negative about his brother's decision to stay at home and minister in local churches, it could be said that this decision helped him to concentrate on writing the thousands of hymns that have built up the worldwide church over the past two and a half centuries. Sally's reluctance to travel is very understandable. She had a young family, was often unwell, and the conditions she had had to endure on the road were atrocious. On the other hand, she had promised that she would support Charles as a travelling preacher, and in some of his letters he virtually begged her to come and see him. It was not easy being the wife of one of the prophets of itinerancy.

It was particularly hard when the other 'prophet of itinerancy' was Charles's brother John, whose wife, Molly, was determined to cause trouble with the in-laws. Charles and Sally worked hard to accept their sister-in-law, sometimes acting as go-betweens in John and Molly's difficult marriage. As well as her constant criticism of her own husband, Molly also felt free to criticize Charles. She publicly declared he was lazy, and blamed him for John's constant travelling. She also seems to have delighted in plaguing Sally, even going so far as to hint at an affair between her and John. On one occasion when Charles was away, he wrote to warn his wife that Molly was also in Bristol – 'I hope Mrs W[esley] keeps her distance. If malice is stronger in her than pride she will pay you a mischievous visit'.[14]

Few women today would even consider putting up with the trials of travelling non-stop eighteenth century style, even temporarily. Sally should be given some credit for trying. She wasn't used to roughing it and she was terrified by the angry mobs who often greeted them, as well as by the frequent thunderstorms. In the following years while Charles was away, she had to cope with the death of five of their eight children, one from smallpox which she also caught and which left her disfigured for life.

On 6 July 1768, she wrote to Charles after the death of their baby John James when he was just four months old:

> *My dear Mr Wesley, this comes to acquaint you that our dear little babe is no more, his agony is over, but it was a hard struggle before he could depart ... glory be to a redeemer's love in declaring (for the consolation of the distressed parents) that 'of such is the kingdom of heaven'. Oh that I may land safely in the harbour of eternal peace!*[15]

As each of her children died, she wrapped a lock of their hair in paper. In one packet she wrote: 'My dear Jacky Wesley's hair: who died of the small-pox, on Monday, Jan. 7th, 1754, aged a year, four months, and seventeen days. I shall go to him; but he shall never return to me.' Charles was often not able to get back in time for his children's funerals. Throughout these trials, she clung to her hope of heaven where she was certain she would meet her children again, and her trust in God's sovereignty. She had refused the offer of the newfangled smallpox vaccination shortly before she and baby Jacky caught the disease. Charles commented in his journal:

> *Mrs. Dewal and Blackwell observed, what a fair opportunity my wife might have had for inoculating with her sister. I answered, that I left every one to his own conscience; but, for my part, I looked upon it as taking the matter out of God's hands; and I should choose, if it depended on me, to trust her entirely to Him.*[16]

Very soon after that he heard that Sally had caught smallpox.

> *Before five I returned to the Foundery, and found two letters from Lady Huntingdon; the first informing me, they apprehended my wife was taken ill of the small-pox, as soon as I left her; the second, that it was come out, and the confluent kind. She had expressed a longing desire to see me, just before I came, and rejoiced for the consolation. I saw her alive; but, O, how changed! The whole head faint, and the whole heart sick! From the crown of the head to the soles of her feet there is no soundness.*

Rather than bitterness at having refused the vaccination, perhaps following her husband's advice, Sally rejoiced. Charles continued:

> *Yet, under her sorest burden, she blessed God that she had not been inoculated; receiving the disease as immediately sent from Him. I found the door of prayer wide open, and entirely acquiesced in the divine will. I would not have it otherwise. God choose for me and mine, in time and eternity![17]*

Sally had lots of wonderful Christian qualities and a vibrant faith. She had many loyal friends who loved and admired her. Selina, Countess of Huntingdon cared for her personally during her bout of smallpox. Sally was generous to a fault; when a servant stole a much-needed £180 from the house, her greatest fear was that she would be expected to press charges.

Unfortunately, her willingness to see the best in everybody and to excuse the faults of others did not help her when it came to parenting. Sally, who had lost five children in infancy and who had a naturally easy-going personality, had a tendency to spoil her three surviving children, Samuel, Sally and Charles. Although Sally junior was a very intelligent and talented child, it was the boys who were particularly indulged. They were both gifted musicians. Samuel, in his autobiography, admitted that they'd got their musical ability from their mother. 'My mother had very considerable vocal talents, played prettily upon the harpsichord and sang sweetly ... My father used to say of my brother and me "The boys have music by the mother's side" meaning that he had no claim to any of the talent that she certainly possessed.'[18]

Sally had clearly been taught singing and the harpsichord as a child, as would have been the norm for the daughter of a wealthy landowner. Having given up so much to marry Charles, she must have been delighted that her sons had inherited her love of music. It was Sally who first encouraged their talent. Charles junior was born in Bristol in December 1757, and his father later wrote:

> *He was two and three quarters old when I first observed his strong inclination to music. He then surprised me by playing a tune on the harpsichord readily and in just time. Soon after he played several, whatever his mother sung or whatever he heard in the streets. From his birth she used to quiet and amuse him with the harpsichord but he would suffer her to play with one hand only taking the other and putting to the keys before he could speak. When he played himself she had to tie him up by his back string to the chair for fear of his falling.[19]*

Samuel was twelve years younger, and his father was nearly sixty by the time he was born. He was even more talented than his older brother. Aged 6 he wrote an oratorio based on the story of the book of Ruth. On its publication two years later, Dr Boyce, a famous musician of the time, commented to his father: 'Sir, I hear you have an English Mozart in your home.'[20] Although Charles encouraged his sons' musical careers, he was often absent, so it was Sally who was largely responsible for bringing them up. Sally was a soft touch and even Charles, who has often been seen as an example of modern, affectionate parenting, encouraged her to be stricter with the children. He wrote: 'I love them as well again as you do, only you make the most of a little love by showing it, and I make the least of a great deal by hiding it.' Perhaps remembering his own mother's concern about the company he and his siblings kept, he wrote: 'It is superfluous, yet I can not help cautioning you about Charles (and Sally too), to take care he contracts no acquaintance with other boys; children are corrupters of each other.'[21]

Whereas Susanna Wesley's main concern was the development of her children's faith, Sally's seems to have been the development of her children's gifts and potential. Although initially Charles had hoped that Charles junior would follow in his footsteps and become a preacher, he soon bowed to the inevitable and accepted that his son would become a musician.

He argued that as his sons would have to earn a living, they needed to be apprenticed in music as they would in any other career. This meant seeking out the very best teachers, at considerable cost. However, by choosing this path, almost certainly encouraged by Sally, Charles was making it more difficult for them to live wholehearted Christian lives. There were no opportunities to develop their musical gifts within Methodism, and to succeed they would need either aristocratic patronage or employment as musicians within the lifeless Church of England.

In 1771, the family moved to London when they were given a large house in a fashionable area rent-free by a Methodist supporter. A few years later, to boost their fame as musical prodigies, a series of concerts featuring Samuel and Charles were organized in their new home. The guest list was a who's who of eighteenth century London. The archbishops of Canterbury and Durham, the Lord Mayor and Lady Mayoress, the famous literary figure Samuel Johnson and vast numbers of lords and ladies paid their subscriptions to hear the young Wesleys perform their own compositions. Although very popular, the results of the concerts were disastrous. They failed to secure Samuel and Charles the aristocratic backing they needed or to win over the influential figures in the Church of England. When Charles applied for the post of organist at St Paul's Cathedral he met with the reply, 'We want no Wesleys here.'

Samuel, in particular, hated being paraded as a child prodigy. He later remarked, 'I hate public life, I always did, and it was a cruel mistake in my education the forcing of me into it.'[22] The concerts and the wealthy circles that the Wesleys now moved in also brought criticism from within the Methodist movement. In 1795, John Fletcher wrote: 'You have your enemies, they complain of your love for music, company, fine people, great folks, and the want of your former zeal and frugality. I need not put you in mind to cut off all sinful appearances.'[23] Sally had been brought up in this world and could not see the problem, but it put up a barrier between her family and the generally much poorer and simpler people that her husband ministered to. As John Wesley commented after one of the concerts, 'I was a little out of my element among lords and ladies. I love plain music and plain company best.'[24]

Sally's mistake in her parenting was to focus on the gift rather than on the Giver. In an attempt to see her children develop their God-given talents, she neglected their spiritual education. Both Charles and Sally junior joined Methodist congregations in later life, but never had the passionate faith of their parents. After their father's death, their uncle John wrote to all of the now adult children to encourage them to claim the gospel for themselves as well as to their mother to warn her about the bad company the 'boys' were keeping. While Charles and Sally were a cause of some concern, Samuel was the real problem. He often stayed out late and came back drunk, and was frequently accused of mistreating the servants. He converted to Roman Catholicism – a real snub to his parents – and when his father tried to end an affair between the 16-year-old Samuel and 22-year-old Charlotte Martin, the relationship between father and son never recovered. Several years later, after his father's death, he shocked society by openly living with Charlotte when they were not married. They did eventually marry when she became pregnant, but he had an affair with a serving girl and Samuel and Charlotte eventually separated.

Sally never gave up on her son and kept in touch throughout this time – often, perhaps unwisely, giving in to his constant requests for money. Interestingly, Samuel did not want his son Charles to stay with his grandmother in London as 'she spoils the boy contrary to his order'.[25] Even he could see that her kindness and generosity were a mixed blessing.

Her brother-in-law John also warned her of the dangers of being too generous. Once Sally was widowed in 1788, after thirty-nine years of marriage, John made sure that she was well looked after. She received a Methodist pension, as well as gifts from supporters including William Wilberforce, but she found it hard to live within her means. John wrote to her:

I know you are of a generous spirit. You have an open heart and an open hand. But may it not sometimes be too open, more so than your circumstances will allow. Is it not an instance of Christian, (as well as worldly) prudence, 'To cut our coat according to our cloth'. If your circumstances are a little narrower should you not contract your expenses too. I need but just give you this hint, which I doubt not you will take kindly.[26]

Sally moved to a smaller house, but otherwise her life continued much as it always had, focused on her children and the church. She lived with Sally and Charles junior, neither of whom married, and her letters mention Samuel and his family coming over for dinner. On one visit to Windsor in 1800, she and Charles 'bumped into' King George III, who invited Charles to play the organ while he chatted to Sally about the importance of music in worship.[27] She clearly still felt comfortable in even the most exalted company! Her daughter commented that even at the age of 89 she was mentally able, had good enough eyesight to read and went out for walks in good weather. Shortly before her death, at the age of 96, she was still attending the annual Methodist General Conference but, to the disappointment of the other delegates, was unable to make a public appearance.

After thirty-four years of widowhood, Sally died in 1822. The description of her death from *The Ladies Repository* of 1867 is a classic pre-Victorian death scene, but still shows the same sure faith and hope of heaven that she clung onto during the many bereavements of her earlier life.

> *The last night she continued to exclaim for an hour 'Open the gates, open the gates!' as in a struggle of soul. Early in the morning she fell into a sweet slumber and awaked with a consoling sense of her Saviour's love a smiling composure so visible on her countenance as to induce a belief that she might rally again. Upon being asked if she found Jesus precious 'O yes!' was her reply. 'And you are happy?' She answered with a serene aspect 'Yes'. After this she spoke little, continuing chiefly silent till the afternoon, gently breathing till without a struggle or groan her spirit passed to the region of light and serenity and love.*[28]

Sally's marriage to Charles was a long and happy one, and her children were all devoted to her. Her sons both became successful and famous musicians, and her daughter Sally was a respected poet. She had a healthy and contented old age, surrounded by friends and family. In many ways her life was a success. However, although she remained a committed Christian throughout her long life, that life was often driven not by her faith, but by the expectations and ambitions that she brought with her from her privileged upbringing. She was prepared to sacrifice a lot when she got married, but when the opportunities arose for the family to live a more prosperous, settled life, mixing with people she felt more at home with, she did not consider the effect on her husband's ministry. When her sons showed remarkable musical gifts, her priority was for them to fulfil their potential, rather than to encourage their spiritual growth. In fact, she was very like many of us. She was a genuine Christian woman, but she allowed herself to be moulded as much by the world as by the Word, as much by her culture as by Christ.

BIBLE STUDY & REFLECTION

Romans 12:1–13

1. What was the 'pattern of this world' *(v. 2)* that Sally had learned from childhood?
   In what ways are you moulded by the 'pattern of this world' that you were brought up with?

2. How does Sally's life show that she had been 'transformed by the renewing of [her] mind' and had godly rather than worldly priorities (v. 2)?

3. In what ways was she still a work in progress? How about you?

4. What were Sally's gifts and how effectively did she use them (vv. 4–8)? What about you?

5. How did her 'afflictions' (v. 12) compare with those you face?

6. How did Sally live out verse 12: 'Be joyful in hope, patient in affliction, faithful in prayer'? How about you?

7. What areas of her life did Sally offer as a 'living sacrifice' (v. 1)? What areas was she less willing to offer wholeheartedly to God?

8. How can you avoid her mistakes?

CHAPTER THREE

Molly Wesley
Bitter, not better

How do you react when life does not turn out the way you had hoped, or when you are let down or disappointed by those closest to you? Do you 'Cast all your anxiety on him because he cares for you',[1] trust in God and His goodness, obey His command to forgive, and grow in knowledge and love of Him? Or do you take the path the world recommends — ignore or blame God, and blame and resent those responsible for your situation, damaging those relationships, and more importantly, damaging your relationship with God? When times are hard, do you grow better, or bitter?

Although Sally Wesley had her faults, she was a paragon of virtue compared to her sister-in-law, Molly. While Susanna Wesley had a character we might aspire to, and Sally had a character we might relate to, the way both contemporaries and biographers have described Molly's character make her sound more like Cruella De Vil than the wife of a respected Christian leader. She was a difficult woman to live with, but she also had difficult circumstances to deal with. We need to see her life as a warning. She was an ordinary human being who reacted to her circumstances in an ungodly way. She was like the man who built his house on sand. Initially, she seemed to be a respectable, able Christian woman. But as she faced the storms in her life, the façade crumbled and she ended up bitter, angry and lonely. She may have listened to Jesus' words, but she didn't act on them. This led to a life that was unstable, unhappy and eventually godless.

Mary, or Molly, seemed quite a suitable match for John Wesley. In 1751 he was 48 and she was 40. Her first husband, Anthony Vazeille, had died a few years earlier, leaving her with four children, a nice house in Threadneedle Street, and a healthy income. Her father and husband had been Huguenots – Protestants who had been forced to leave France following persecution under Louis XIV. They had found their spiritual home with the Methodists in London, and Molly was very involved in church activities. The family was friendly with the Perronets, who also had a Huguenot background, and who were close friends of the Wesley brothers. She was a mature, competent, apparently Christian woman, who was unlikely to have more children and so hinder John's itinerant ministry. She appeared to be a sensible choice to be the wife of John Wesley, the 'high priest of Methodism'.

John Wesley, however, was unlikely to have been a sensible choice of husband for anybody. He had been convinced that all Methodist preachers should be single, and throughout his life he continued to teach younger ministers the value of celibacy. Just before his marriage, he told a friend that he had told Molly that he would not 'preach one sermon, or travel one mile less on that account'.[2] His reluctance to marry was not due to a dislike of women. His sister Hetty told him that he liked 'woman merely for being woman'.[3] He loved their company and from early adulthood he had close, even romantic, friendships with women. The letters he wrote could be very passionate, although he always claimed that he was only offering spiritual support. James Hutton wrote in his memoirs in 1740: 'Both John and Charles Wesley are dangerous snares to many young women. Several are in love with them. I wish they were married to some good sisters, though I would not give them one of mine, even if I had many ...'[4]

At a Methodist conference in 1748, John was persuaded that his ministry would be more, rather than less effective if he married. He became more convinced once Charles had broken the brothers' vow of singleness and married in 1749, and after he met the woman who he felt would perfectly complement his ministry. Unfortunately that woman was not Molly.

Grace Murray was a young widow from Newcastle. She had been a domestic servant and had married a sailor. She started attending Methodist meetings following the death of a child, while her husband was away at sea. After a rocky start, and initial opposition from her husband, she became a committed and gifted Christian worker. Following her husband's death at sea she helped to run the Methodist orphanage, cared for travelling preachers who fell ill, and had over a hundred women in her Bible classes. When Wesley needed nursing on one of his many trips up north, she personally cared for him, and he became convinced that she was the woman he should marry. He proposed and she seemed to accept. He later described the proposal.

The night before I left Newcastle I told her 'I am convinced God had call'd you to be my Fellow Labourer in the gospel. I will take you with me to Ireland in Spring. Now we must part for a time. But if we meet again, I trust we shall part no more.'[5]

However, things were more complicated than they appeared. Grace had previously cared for another convalescing preacher called John Bennett, who was also expecting to marry her. Grace couldn't make up her mind. According to John, she was 'under racking uncertainty of mind. When she received a letter from me, she resolved to live and die with me and wrote to me just what she felt. When she heard from him, her affection for him revived and she wrote to him in the tenderest manner'.[6] Nonetheless, she did spend the next few months travelling in Ireland with John and helping him with his ministry. John wrote: 'She lighted my burden more than can be expected. She examined all the women in the smaller Societies and the believers in every place ... [she] visited the sick; prayed with the mourners ... she told me with all faithfulness and freedom if she thought anything amiss in my behaviour'.[7]

Things were going so well, but then they returned to England where Grace heard gossip about Wesley's friendship with another young woman. Upset, she wrote to Bennett, and their relationship was back on. John's brother Charles soon got involved as well, convinced that John marrying would damage his ministry, and that if he were to marry anyone it should not be Grace – she had been a servant girl, after all, and Charles believed she had promised to marry Bennett first. He encouraged Grace and Bennett to get married. When John heard the news, he was heartbroken. He had been certain that Grace was his soul mate whom God had chosen for him to marry; anybody else was bound to be second best.

That second best choice was Molly Vazeille. Having decided that God wanted him to marry, John Wesley now just needed a wife. This time he was not going to mention his plans to Charles, who he blamed for his loss of Grace Murray. However, this time a bit of brotherly advice would have been very helpful. Charles already knew Molly and had not been impressed. He had met her at their friends', the Perronets'. He and Sally had even taken her to his in-laws' new home in Chepstow, and stayed with her in Threadneedle Street for over a week. He described Molly as having a 'sorrowful spirit'. The general opinion of her was more favourable. John's friend Henry Moore later wrote:

> From all that I have heard from Mr Wesley and others, (she) had every appearance of being well qualified for the sphere into which she was introduced. She seemed truly pious, and was very agreeable in her person and manners. She conformed to every company whether of the rich or the poor: and she had a remarkable facility and propriety in addressing them concerning their true interests.[8]

This was the side that John saw. He knew Molly a little, and had written to her in the previous year – a far less intimate letter than he wrote to several other female correspondents. There was no hint that he had thought of marrying her until a couple of weeks before the wedding; she isn't even mentioned in his journal as a friend.

But for some reason John decided that Molly was now to be the woman he should marry. He wrote to her that he had been impressed by 'your indefatigable industry, your exact frugality, your uncommon neatness and cleanness, both in your person and all things round you'[9] It doesn't sound very romantic, but John was obsessively tidy, so such things were obviously important to him.

On 9 February 1751, a marriage contract was drawn up. Again, not very romantically, John promised that he would not touch her fortune, nor would Molly be responsible for any of John's debts. John had then planned to go on a preaching trip, but had hurt his foot slipping on ice. Unable to travel, he convalesced at Molly's house where she nursed him, and ten days later they were married – an event that is not mentioned at all in his journal. Charles was one of the last to hear the news. He was horrified. He wrote in his journal: 'I was thunderstruck, and could only answer that he had given me the first blow, and his marriage would come like the coup de grâce ... I refused his company to the chapel and retired to mourn with my faithful Sally.'[10] John, still suffering from his injured foot, immediately left for the planned preaching tour.

Although the marriage was hardly love's young dream, there was no reason for it not to work. Molly had been successfully married before. She had inherited her husband's wealth and house and so, unlike many widows at the time, she did not need to remarry for financial security. Presumably she wanted to marry John, and to make the marriage a success. She had been used to being alone for long periods when her first husband went on business trips abroad – often for months at a time. John's frequent absences would be nothing new. Despite the very practical nature of the marriage agreement, John too seemed to want to build a warm, affectionate relationship with his new wife. His early letters are very loving. A month after getting married, he wrote:

> *My dear Molly, – Do I write too soon? Have not you above all the people in the world a right to hear from me as soon as possibly I can? You have surely a right to every proof of love I can give and to all the little help which is in my power. For you have given me even your own self. O how can we praise God enough for making us helps meet for each other! I am utterly astonished at His*

goodness. Let not only our lips but our lives show forth His praise![11]

A week or so later, he wrote:

Last night I had the pleasure of receiving Two Letters, from my Dearest Earthly Friend. I can't answer them, till I tell you, How I love you: Though you knew it before. You feel it in your own breast. For (Thanks be to God) your Heart is as my Heart. And in token of it, you have given me your Hand.[12]

Initially, the marriage appeared to be working. Molly travelled with John when she could. In March 1752, they set off travelling to Birmingham, Manchester, Bristol, Leeds, Epworth, Grimsby, York, Durham, Newcastle, Penrith, Cockermouth and Whitehaven. On 13 July they travelled to Ireland, only returning in October. During this trip, John wrote from Epworth: 'After taking a round of between three and four hundred miles we came hither yesterday in the afternoon. My wife is at least as well as when she left London. The more she travels the better she bears it.'[13] When left at home, she helped with the Methodist accounts and later helped organize the Methodist publishing business. She had business experience from her first marriage which she used to help the church. She was also accepted and valued by the wider church family. John wrote to her:

NEWCASTLE-UPON-TYNE May 22, 1752. MY DEAR LOVE, — Give the glory to God. Your name is precious among this people. They talk of you much and know not how to commend you enough, even for those little things, your plainness of dress, your sitting among the poor at the preaching, your using sage-tea and not being delicate in your food. Their way of mentioning you often brings tears into my eyes. Bless God for all His benefits.[14]

Molly was the ideal minister's wife. So what went wrong? Despite John's affectionate letters he was an inconsiderate husband. He was in his late forties and was set in his ways. He was unable to appreciate how hard it would be for Molly to adapt to being married to him. In the same letter in which John had gushed that 'your Heart is as my Heart', he bluntly demanded that Molly should give up her family home. 'You will quit your House ... at Midsummer. We agree, in desiring to cut off every needless expense.'[15]

When Molly married him she had four children. The youngest, Noah, was only 4 years old and had never known his father. We know he was baptized in St Helen's Bishopsgate in 1747, the year Anthony Vazeille died. John didn't consider the children when he expected Molly to travel with him. Jenny, her young daughter, went with her mother when she travelled the country with her husband, and had to put up with the same dreadful conditions and threats of violence. Even John's brother Charles, who never got on with Molly, sympathized with her. He wrote to his wife, Sally in 1755: 'I pity his poor wife, if now upon the road. There she is likely to stick until the warm weather comes. The roads are almost impassable for wheels.'[16]

The boys, even little Noah, were sent away to school. When they became dangerously ill, John was not very sympathetic. He wrote to a friend: 'My wife set off for Bristol last week. I hope her fears will prove groundless and that all her children will live to glorify God.'[17] When one of her sons was dying, it never crossed John's mind to accompany her. 'My wife, desiring to pay the last office to her poor dying child, set out for London, and came a few days before he went home.'[18] The children were not his own, but John's attitude was harsh, and shows little understanding of his wife's feelings. It seems unlikely that John's marriage would have been a happy one, whoever he had married.

John may have been inconsiderate, but Molly's reaction made things far worse. From the start she moaned. On marrying the famous John Wesley she had expected status and respect. She got neither. As she travelled, she had to put up with the same basic conditions that John had grown used to, and in places John's adoring female fans resented her as his wife. When after four years on the road Molly decided to stay at home, John was relieved. He, rather disloyally, wrote to a friend:

> *In my last journey into the North, all my patience was put to the proof again and again; and all my endeavours to please, but without success. In my present journey I leap as broke from chains. I am content with whatever entertainment I meet with, and my companions are always in good humour 'because "they are with me"'. This must be the spirit of all who take journeys with me. If a dinner is ill dressed, or a hard bed, a poor room, a shower of rain, or a dusty road will put them out of humour it lays a burthen upon me greater than all the rest put together ... to hear persons at my ear fretting and murmuring at everything is tike [sic] tearing the flesh off my bones.[19]*

Travelling together had not brought them closer. But if John thought that absence would make the heart grow fonder, he was mistaken. Having met many of John's female admirers on her travels, Molly became more and more concerned about what John was getting up to without her. A few months after they were married, John rather naively encouraged Molly to open all his correspondence while he was away. He wrote to her: 'If any letter comes to you addressed to the Revd John Wesley, open it. It is for yourself. Dear Love Adieu.'[20] This might have helped Molly run the publishing business and deal with money matters, but it certainly didn't help their relationship. She opened his post and was horrified by what she found. She read letters from women who appeared to have much more intimate friendships with her husband than she did.

Molly's imagination ran riot. She had always been jealous. Only three months after the wedding, John was worried about her. 'My wife, upon all supposition that I did not love her, and that I trusted others more than her, had often fretted herself almost to death.'[21] John did nothing to allay her fears. He insisted on his right to see and write to whoever he pleased – and some of his letters were definitely open to misinterpretation.

The woman who eventually caused Molly most pain was Sarah Ryan. She had a colourful past and was married simultaneously to two, or even three, men. She became a Christian in 1754 and controversially, only three years later, John appointed her to be the housekeeper of the Methodist school at Kingswood near Bristol. John was very fond of her and wrote her affectionate and indiscreet letters, sometimes even writing complaints about his wife.

February 10 1756 My Dear Sister, Your last letter was seasonable indeed. I was growing faint in my mind. The being continually watched over for evil; the having every word I spoke, every action I did small and great watched over with no friendly eye; the hearing a thousand little tart unkind reflections in return for the kindest words I could devise ... 'Like drops of eating water on the marble, At length have worn my sinking spirits down' ... Yet I could not say Take thy plague away from me, but only Let me be purified not consumed.[22]

Molly was convinced they were having an affair, and on one trip to Bristol, while Sarah was serving a group of visiting preachers, Molly exploded, yelling, 'The whore now serving you has three husbands living!' When she discovered one of the letters, enough was enough, and she left her husband. John wrote to Sarah to explain what happened.

1758 MY DEAR SISTER Last Friday after many severe words my wife left me, vowing she would see me no more. As I had wrote to you the same morning I began to reason with myself till I almost doubted whether I had done well in writing or whether I ought to write to you at all. After prayer that doubt was taken away. Yet I was almost sorry that I had written that morning. In the evening while I was preaching at the chapel she came into the chamber where I had left my clothes, searched my pockets and found the letter there which I had finished but had not sealed. While she read it God broke her heart and I afterward found her in such a temper as I have not seen her in for several years. She has continued in the same ever since.

John could not see that he had done anything wrong. It was always Molly who was being unreasonable. He wrote to her:

I insist on choosing my own company! ... I insist upon conversing, by speaking or writing, with those whom I (not you) judge proper. For more than seven years this has been a bone of contention between you and me, and it is so still, for I will not, I can not, I dare not give it up.[23]

In many ways, up to this point, our sympathy may well be with Molly. She had a very difficult husband who never considered her needs or interests, and for whom the demands of gospel ministry trumped all other responsibilities. He always believed he was right and, as he was a respected religious leader, there were few who would support her. When his friend Ebenezer Blackwell tried to mediate between the warring couple, John was furious that he seemed to be taking her side.

Moaning and even jealousy might appear natural, if not particularly godly, reactions to the situation. Unfortunately, moaning and jealousy were not Molly's only reactions. Although over the years there were temporary reconciliations, Molly and John's marriage went from bad to worse. He stubbornly refused to change his behaviour, and rather than humbly accepting the situation she reacted increasingly bitterly. In the letter above, John continues:

> *But then you will rage and fret and call me names. I am sorry for it, but I can not help it ... Be it so, but still I stand just where I was. Then you will 'show my private letters to the world.' If you do I must assert my right still.*[24]

Molly did indeed 'rage and fret and call [him] names' publicly as well as privately. John's brother Charles described an occasion when Molly locked them in a room to tell them both all their faults. Charles only survived the experience by reciting Latin poetry to drown her out! There is one report of a visitor arriving to find Molly dragging John around the room by his hair.[25] She was convinced that John was being unfaithful, and was said to travel a hundred miles to check that he was travelling alone. At one time she dismantled his bed and rebuilt it in his (very small) study. John had earlier encouraged her to open his letters so that she could help with his business affairs. She now opened all his letters intending to cause mischief. When he locked his desk to stop her, she broke into it and stole them. When things got really bad, she went even further. She did 'show [his] private letters to the world'. At a time when the followers of Wesley and those of George Whitefield were in profound disagreement on the issue of free will, she made the most of the split and handed over John's letters to female friends for his enemies to publish. Thankfully his 'enemies' bore less of a grudge towards John than his wife did. Charles's daughter Sally wrote:

About this time Mrs Wesley had obtained some letters which she used to the most injurious purposes misinterpreting spiritual expressions and interpolating words. These she read to some Calvinists and they were to be sent to the Morning Post. A Calvinist gentleman who esteemed my father and uncle came to the former and told him that for the sake of religion the publication should be stopped and Mr John Wesley be allowed to answer for himself. As Mrs Wesley had read, but did not show, the letters to him he had some doubts of their authenticity and though they were addressed to Mr John Wesley they might be forgeries.[26]

———————◆•◆•◆———————

Molly was determined to do what she could to destroy her husband's ministry. Fortunately for John, and unfortunately for Molly, no one took her side. Whereas initially she was accepted by the Methodist congregations, she became increasingly isolated. There were still times when John and Molly were living together, and she was apparently involved in ministry with him. John notes in his journal in 1772 that he was travelling through Yorkshire and 'calling at a little inn on the moors, I spoke a few words to an old man there, as did my wife to the woman of the house'.[27] However, her reputation was damaged and she was disliked by many of her husband's friends.

When Molly was left on her own in Bristol, the local Methodists seemed to delight in making her life a misery. She wrote to John, 'The very day you set off from Bristol [Mrs Madan] said "I hope Mrs Wesley is not to stay here till Mr Wesley returns, for if she does the society will be ruined."'[28] She continued, 'My dear friend, let me beg of you for God's sake, for your own sake, put a stop to this torrent of evil that is poured out against me. It is cruel to make me an offender for defending myself.' She had alienated Charles and Sally Wesley early on. She went to live with her daughter

Jenny at least once when she left John, but as she was married to a prominent Methodist preacher in Newcastle, she was unlikely to have given her mother unconditional support.

Had Molly been more accepted into Methodist circles – as she had been before her marriage – she might have had friends who could have helped her to respond to her difficult marriage in a more godly way. It did not help that everyone seemed unquestioningly to accept John's version of events, which were not exactly objective. The only spiritual 'help' she got was from him, and it often wasn't that helpful. Here is one example of his advice to his wife.

I can not but add a few words, not by way of reproach, but of advice. God had used many means to break your stubborn will and curb the impetuosity of your temper. He has given you a dutiful, but sickly daughter. He has taken away one of your sons; another has been a grievous cross, the third probably will be; he has suffered you to be defrauded of much money. He has chastened you with strong pain [Molly suffered from severe gout]; and still he may say 'How long liftest thou up thyself against me?' Are you more humble, more patient, more placable than you were before? I fear quite the reverse ...[29]

Criticizing someone's children is rarely a good idea, and Molly was never going to listen to advice from John when he was totally blind to his own failings.

She should have listened to his advice early on in their marriage, before things were beyond repair. John wrote an affectionate letter just a month after the wedding, which also included instructions on various business matters. He ended by writing, 'Let no business of any kind hinder the intercourse between God and your soul! Neither let anything prevent your spending at least one hour a day in private reading, prayer, and meditation.'[30] He was already worried that she lacked real, personal faith.

As the years went by, and her troubles increased, rather than learning to trust in Christ, like Susanna, and grow in godliness, she grew bitter and vengeful. She had a difficult marriage, as her mother-in-law had done, but while Susanna was building her house on rock, Molly had built hers on sand. Susanna survived the storm. Molly did not. When she died in 1781, John only found out several days after the funeral. His reflection on the marriage was noted by his friend Henry Moore, who commented that if Mrs Wesley had been a better wife, John would have spent more time at home, and less in ministry.[31]

BIBLE STUDY & REFLECTION

Romans 12:14 –21

1. In what ways could Molly be said to have been persecuted (v. 14)?

2. How far did her response match that encouraged in verse 14?

3. Verse 15 encourages us to empathize with others — why did Molly find that so hard? Why might we?

4. Why did Molly find it so hard to 'live in harmony' with John (v. 16)?

5. Who do you find it hardest to live in harmony with? Why?

6. What were the results of Molly choosing to repay 'evil for evil' (v. 17)?

7. Why are we tempted to take revenge rather than 'leave room for God's wrath' (v. 19)?

8. How can we make sure we are the sort of people who love our enemies (v. 20) and 'overcome evil with good' (v. 21)?

CHAPTER FOUR

Elizabeth Whitefield
A marriage made
in heaven?

What should a Christian marriage look like? It's an important question, because getting it wrong can lead to unrealistic expectations leading to disillusionment and divorce. Many Christians in the twenty-first century have very similar views on marriage to their non- Christian friends. Marriage, to them, should be based on physical attraction and romantic love, and should be a relationship where it is each partner's job to meet the other's needs. When any of those factors are no longer present, the marriage is at an end. But what if that is not God's view of marriage? The Bible gives us a picture of marriage as a relationship of sacrifice, commitment and forgiveness, rather than merely passion and romance. God alone can meet our real need for love, support and acceptance, whether we are married or single. A marriage can be 'made in heaven' – used by God for His glory and the holiness of His people – whether it fits the Hollywood criteria of a happy marriage or not.

In twenty-first century terms, Elizabeth Whitefield's marriage looks disastrous. Like Molly Wesley, Elizabeth was a widow and the second-choice wife of a travelling preacher. The signs didn't look good, particularly as he was also her second-choice husband. Not surprisingly, she was bracketed together with Molly Wesley in the minds of some contemporaries.

John Berridge, the eccentric vicar of Everton, wrote about the marriages of his friends, the Wesley brothers and George Whitefield: 'Matrimony has quite marred poor Charles, and might have spoiled John and George, if a wise master had not graciously sent them a brace of ferrets.'[1]

That Molly and Elizabeth were bracketed together in people's minds was largely down to the testimony of one man – Cornelius Winter. He lived with the Whitefields on and off for a couple of years towards the end of Elizabeth's life, and his description of their life together has been endlessly repeated. He wrote: 'He was not happy in his wife ... He did not intentionally make his wife unhappy. He always presented great decency and decorum in his conduct towards her. Her death set his mind much at liberty. She did not certainly behave in all respect as she ought.'[2] These few blunt words did untold damage to Elizabeth's reputation. The marriage is shown as cold and loveless, based on 'decency and decorum', not affection and respect, and a burden that Whitefield was relieved to be rid of when Elizabeth died. Perhaps if he had looked at more than just the last months of their life together, Winter might have come to a different conclusion.

Whitefield was the youngest of the three leaders of the Evangelical Revival. He was a very religious young man from a humble background. He became a member of the Wesleys' Holy Club in Oxford, which wasn't much help in his search for spiritual growth. He only understood the gospel of grace after having damaged his health fasting in an attempt to conquer sin. He later wrote: 'I know the place ... Whenever I go to Oxford, I cannot help running to the spot where Jesus Christ first revealed himself to me and gave me the new birth.' It took John and Charles Wesley a failed missionary trip to Georgia and several more years before they understood the same message. George also started preaching outdoors well before the Wesleys. In his lifetime it is estimated he preached to over ten million people, and that during his many trips to the American colonies, every man, woman and child had heard him preach at least once. He was a very busy and single-minded man, but unlike the Wesleys, he decided to get married relatively early, when he was in his mid-twenties.

This did not mean he was a romantic. In fact, he was determined that romance should play no part whatsoever in his wedding plans. Nowadays there is a universal assumption, even in Christian circles, that almost the sole basis for marriage is romantic love. When that initial feeling 'dies', the marriage is assumed to be over. The mid-eighteenth century was where this idea began. It was a time when emotion was becoming more and more important in cultural and personal life. Whitefield himself was criticized by the established church for his emotional preaching, which often left his hearers weeping, and romantic love was replacing economic and social factors as a reason for getting married.

Despite, or perhaps because of, his passionate character, Whitefield was determined to resist the trend of marrying for love. He believed that romance could cause the loved one to become an idol, and should play no part in marriage. His motives were far more practical. He had seen successful Christian marriages at first-hand, and saw how they could help the husband's ministry. While in America he had stayed with Jonathan and Sarah Edwards, and described the family.

A sweeter couple I have not yet seen. Their children were dressed not in silks and satins but plain as becomes the children of those who in all things ought to be examples of Christian simplicity. She is adorned with a meek and quiet spirit, talked feelingly and solidly of the things of God, and seemed to be such a helpmate for her husband that she caused me to renew those prayers, which for some months I had put up to God, that he would be pleased to send me a daughter of Abraham to be my wife.[3]

He had also been impressed by the love and support that his friend Edmund Jones was given by his wife over a long life in ministry. Whitefield seems to have ignored the fact that both couples were devoted to each other, and that romantic love had played an important part in bringing them together. He also had a more pressing reason to get married. He needed a female helper in his work. He had set up an orphanage in Georgia, and he was finding it difficult to find women to look after the children in such an isolated place in the colony. Could a marriage based on such pragmatic foundations ever succeed?

George initially proposed to a woman called Elizabeth Delamotte. She came from a wealthy Methodist family, and although he knew she would have to sacrifice a great deal in marrying him, he believed that she was the woman God had chosen. While he was travelling in America, he wrote to her parents asking for their permission to marry their daughter, and included another letter with the proposal for Elizabeth herself. To her parents he wrote that he was 'free from that foolish passion which the world calls love' and

> *I write only because I believe it is the will of God that I should alter my state; but your denial will fully convince me that your daughter is not the person appointed by God for me. He knows my heart; I would not marry but for Him, and in Him, for ten thousand worlds.*[4]

In his proposal to Elizabeth, he described what marriage to him would be like – the loneliness, hardship, hard work, poverty and sacrifice. He was realistic, but it did not sound an attractive prospect. Again he stressed that it was not a romantic proposal: 'The passionate expressions which carnal courtiers use, I think ought to be avoided by those that marry in the Lord.'[5] It is possible that he genuinely cared for her. It was not the impression that the letter gave. Not surprisingly, Elizabeth Delamotte turned him down.

That soon after Elizabeth James accepted him is more surprising. Elizabeth number two was in love with another man. Howell Harris, a close friend of Whitefield's and a leader of the revival in Wales, was also in love with her. Harris, however, had decided that he should not marry, and so suggested that she should marry his friend George. When it became clear that Harris was serious about the idea, and that Elizabeth had no hope of marrying the man she loved, she eventually agreed to the plan. She was a middle-aged widow, working as a housekeeper who, in giving up Harris, probably thought that any hope of future happiness had ended.

Having been rejected by his own choice, Elizabeth Delamotte, Whitefield was quite content to leave the matchmaking to his friend. Although she was ten years older than George, she was a suitable choice. She had become a Christian three years earlier, and was liked and respected by John Wesley, who a month before the wedding called her a 'woman of candour and humanity'[6] Whitefield didn't know her well, and before the wedding there was no mention of her in his letters. He rode 300 miles from Scotland, where he was conducting a mission, to Abergavenny in Wales, where she lived. Shortly after he arrived, they got married – 14 November 1741. Howell Harris gave her away at the wedding!

George wrote to a friend about his new wife: 'The Lord has given me a wife. Her name was James, a widow, between thirty and forty years of age. She has been a housekeeper many years. Once gay; but for three years last past a despised follower of the Lamb of God.'[7] A few weeks later he wrote to another friend:

About eleven weeks ago I married in the fear of God one who was a widow, of about thirty six years of age, and who has been a housekeeper for many years; neither rich in fortune, nor beautiful as to her person, but, I believe a true child of God, and one who would not, I think, attempt to hinder me in His work for the world. In that respect I am just the same as before marriage. I hope God will never suffer me to say 'I have married a wife and therefore I cannot come.'[8]

He hoped that Elizabeth would help, not hinder him in his ministry. 'As I married for the Lord, I trust I shall not thereby be hindered, but rather forwarded, in my work.'[9]

Like John Wesley, George had no intention of travelling or preaching any less than he had before he got married. Three days after the wedding he was on the road again. As George's ministry was as much in America as it was in the British Isles, travelling with him would mean even more discomfort and danger than it had for Molly and Sally Wesley. For Elizabeth, choosing to stay at home would mean far longer separations, with fewer letters and little news of her husband. Unlike Molly and Sally, she had no family money to supplement the very meagre income of a travelling preacher, and so was destined to a life of poverty. Add to all of that, her heartbreak at losing Howell Harris, who she said she continued to be in love with for the next ten years. Howell and George stayed close friends, constantly wrote to each other and met up when they could, which must have made the situation even harder to bear.

One advantage that Elizabeth had over Molly was that Whitefield's relationships with other women were beyond reproach. His pastoral letters to women really were strictly pastoral, and although he was adored by thousands of women who heard him preach, there were never any rumours or suspicions about his behaviour. Even so, Elizabeth's life as Mrs Whitefield was not going to be easy.

Very soon, Elizabeth saw the gritty reality of George's work. Having started preaching outdoors to coal miners near Bristol, he continued wherever he went – sometimes it was because the crowds were too great to fit into churches, sometimes because the church authorities banned him from their pulpits, and sometimes because he wanted to preach wherever crowds of people gathered. Whitefield regularly preached to tens of thousands of people at a time. Often the crowds gathered specifically to hear what he had to say, but he could also meet with real hostility.

In London just a few months after he got married, he decided to preach at the fairgrounds that were set up over the Easter holidays. The crowds were there for the fair, not for preaching; the stallholders were there to make money, and resented anyone who would distract their customers. George preached at the Moorfields fair, and despite some heckling, many listened. The next day he went to Marylebone Fields. Bare-fisted boxing was one of the attractions, and as George started to speak, the boxers threatened to attack his pulpit. He stalled, and was tempted to leave until Elizabeth tugged at his cloak and encouraged him to keep going. He carried on, even though stones and rubbish were hurled at him. Their marriage may have not been a love match, but in some ways she complemented him perfectly. Whitefield admitted to being physically cowardly – Elizabeth was brave. Her courage and encouragement clearly impressed him. He mentioned it when he preached at her funeral.

Do you remember my preaching in those fields by the old stump of a tree? The multitude was great, and many were disposed to be riotous. At first I addressed them firmly; but when a desperate gang drew near, with the most ferocious and horrid imprecations and menaces, my courage began to fail. My wife was then standing beside me as I stood on the table. I think I hear her now. She pulled my gown, and, looking up, said 'George, play the man for your God.'[10]

Money was another problem to cope with. They never had enough. George was used to having very little and never complained, but for Elizabeth, who had been a housekeeper in what must have been quite a wealthy household, it must have been difficult. George bought some second-hand curtains for their home and, as they could not afford any furniture, they had to borrow from a friend. George wrote to thank him: 'I thank you a thousand times for your great generosity in lending me some furniture, having little of my own. I know who will repay you.'[11] Immediately after the baptism of their son, Elizabeth and the baby had to leave London to save money. George explained the situation in another letter: 'Housekeeping being expensive in London, I thought it best to send both parent and child to Abergavenny where my wife had a little house, the furniture of which, as I thought of soon embarking for Georgia, I had partly sold and partly given away.'[12] It doesn't sound like the ideal home for a new baby.

Unfortunately they never reached Abergavenny. Whitefield's letter continued:

In their journey thither, they stopped at Gloucester, at the Bell Inn, which my brother now keeps, and in which I was born. There my beloved was struck off with a stroke. Upon my coming here, without knowing what happened, I enquired concerning the welfare of parent and child, and, by the answer, found that the flower was cut down.

The Whitefield's baby son John was dead. He was just four months old. George was devastated. He had hoped that the baby would grow up to be a great preacher, and after the child's death, he worried that God had taken his son from him as he had been tempted to love him too much and for him to become his idol. Elizabeth must have been grief-stricken too. It is possible that Whitefield was partly responsible for his son's death. Just a few weeks before the birth, the couple were involved in a dreadful accident. George was driving. He described what happened in a letter to a friend.

My wife has been in trying circumstances, partly through the unskilfulness of a chaise driver;— I mean myself. Being advised to take her out into the air, I drove her, as well as myself, through inadventure into a ditch. The ditch might be about fourteen feet deep. All who saw us cried out 'They are killed', but through infinite mercy we received no great hurt. The place was very narrow near the bottom, and yet the horse went down, as though lowered on a pulley. A bystander ran and caught hold of its head to prevent it going forward. I got up on its back and was drawn out whilst my wife, still hanging between the chaise and the bank, was pulled up by two or three assistants.

———————————◆•◆•◆———————————

 George did not expect the baby to be born imminently, as he continued, 'Not expecting my wife's delivery for some time, I intend making a short excursion.'[13] While he was away, the baby arrived. It seems likely that the birth was premature, possibly as a result of these traumatic events. John was Elizabeth's only child. She had no children from her first marriage, and when John died she was nearly 40. Although she was pregnant several times, each time she miscarried, and her final pregnancy ended in a stillbirth.

Despite the tragedy of baby John's death, they still kept to their plan of travelling to America, where Elizabeth was to help run the Bethesda orphanage. They left from Plymouth in August 1744, and arrived in New Hampshire eleven weeks later. The voyage made the Wesley brothers' trips around the British Isles look very tame. After they arrived, Whitefield was so ill that he asked his wife to write to supporters at home on his behalf. She wrote:

My dear and honoured master has ordered me to send you an account of our sorrowful, yet joyful, voyage. Our captain and others say they never saw such a voyage; for all nature seemed to be upside down. We had nothing but storms, calms and contrary winds. We frequently expected to go into eternity. Our own provision was spent and Mr Whitefield was so ill, that he could not take the ship's provision.[14]

Later in the journey, Whitefield was so hungry that he ate raw potatoes, which made him very unwell. Elizabeth doesn't even mention one of the most frightening parts of the voyage, when the captain and crew believed they were about to be attacked by enemy ships. George described what happened: 'All except my self seemed ready for fire and smoke. My wife, having dressed herself to prepare for all events, set about making cartridges, whilst I wanted to go into the holes of the ship, hearing that was the chaplain's usual place.'[15] Even though it was a false alarm, once again it was Elizabeth who acted bravely in a threatening situation. The 'holes of the ship' may have been the 'chaplain's usual place', but being 'prepare[d] for all events' and making cartridges seems a far braver and more practical response in the face of an enemy attack.

Things weren't much easier once they had arrived in

America. George insisted on preaching constantly, even though his friends believed he was dying. He was very touched by their concern, and even wrote a little poem:

My wife and friends stood weeping by,
In tears resolved to see me die[16]

Faced with George's packed timetable and aware of his phenomenal gifts and popularity as a preacher, it would have been understandable for Elizabeth to feel resentful and inadequate. In fact, she supported him and made herself as useful as she could, however menial the task. While George preached, Elizabeth copied his letters for him. It was a happy time. George wrote, 'My wife and I go on like a pair of happy pilgrims, leaning upon our Beloved.'[17] Eventually, a year later, they travelled to the orphanage, where Elizabeth was to use her experience as a housekeeper. The little group had to ride, and sometimes walk, through 700 miles of largely uncharted forest to reach Bethesda. They arrived in December 1745, and intended to spend the winter together. Whitefield discovered on arrival that, as usual, the orphanage was in desperate need of funds, and so a few weeks later he was off again – preaching and fundraising – leaving Elizabeth to cope alone. He was always on the road, passing through Bethesda when he could. That summer he found Elizabeth very unwell, following her fourth and final miscarriage and suffering from the intense Georgian heat and humidity. He realized she needed to be moved to a more comfortable climate.

> *The summer season being so far advanced, I think it most advisable to go by water and so return to the southward when the weather is cooler — My dear wife has been very ill — Blessed be GOD she is now better; but dares not stay here in the heat of summer — All Friends think it would kill her. She will therefore come with me and in the mean while joins in sending most cordial salutations to you and yours and all our dear, very dear Boston friends.*[18]

Her health never fully recovered. Nevertheless, George soon left her at Bethesda again, while he returned to England. He had meant to return, but she was on her own in America from February 1747 to June 1749. He was aware of the difficulty of her situation. A year after he left he wrote to his and her friend, Howell Harris, 'My dear wife will have a trial in my being absent so long.'[19] After receiving donations for his work, while in Bermuda, en route to England, he wrote in his journal '[they] have raised me upwards of a hundred pounds sterling. This will pay a little of Bethesda's debt, and enable me to make such a remittance to my dear yoke fellow, as may keep her from being embarrassed, or too much beholden in my absence.'[20] He didn't come back and, after more than two years, she had had enough and sailed for home.

From then on, she stayed in London while George travelled on both sides of the Atlantic. He understood that she would find this hard, and encouraged friends to visit her while he was away. He wrote from Lisbon, en route to America once more: 'Pray for me, and add to my obligations by frequently visiting my poor wife. Kindnesses shown to her, during my absence will be a double kindness.'[21] And again, 'You will not forget to visit my widow wife! Blessed be God, her maker is her husband and ere long we shall all sit down together, at the marriage supper of the lamb.'[22] Despite his concern for her he continued his punishing routine of travelling and preaching. He was once tempted to return early when he heard she was dangerously ill. 'I thought my wife's illness would have hastened me to London; but as she is now recovering I would fain proceed in my summer's campaign.'[23] He kept to his word made when he got married: 'I hope God will never suffer me to say, 'I have married a wife, and therefore I cannot come.'''

Elizabeth found those long months of separation hard. She suffered from poor health, and soon after her return from America, after a difficult pregnancy, she lost another child. George wrote from the home of Selina, Countess of Huntingdon in 1750: 'I am now waiting every day for my wife's being delivered of her present burden, and hope ere long to rejoice that a child is born into the world. O that it might be born again and be made an heir to the redeemer's kingdom.'[24] There are no other references to the child; just worries about Elizabeth's health – she was 45. A few months later, George wrote: 'My wife has been in pitiable circumstances for some time. The Lord only knows what will be the issue of them. This is my comfort. "All things work together for good to those who love God." He is the Father of all mercies and God of all consolation.'[25]

Over the following years there are numerous mentions of Elizabeth's being unwell, but at times she was well enough to meet friends and attend important events. She was present at the trial in Westminster Hall of Earl Ferrers, the cousin of the Countess of Huntingdon, who was accused of murdering his steward in 1760. To support their friend the countess, George and Elizabeth went to the trial with Sally and Charles Wesley. It was a bizarre and glittering occasion. Charles Wesley described the event in his journal:

> *The lords entered with the utmost state: first the barons, then the lords, bishops, earls, dukes and Lord High Steward. Most of the royal family, the peeresses, and chief gentry of the kingdom, and the foreign ambassadors were present, and made*

it one of the most august assemblies in Europe.[26]

For a housekeeper from Wales, it must have been an amazing experience. The earl, who was obviously mad, was convicted, and Whitefield visited him in prison several times before he was hanged.

Elizabeth had a close relationship with Selina, Countess of Huntingdon, and in an extraordinary letter, written shortly after the loss of her child, we get a rare glimpse of her personality and what made her tick. She explained that she had not written sooner because 'I was in bed when I received your ladyship's letter, and was not able to read it. I had a pleuritic fever, and was so low that the doctor durst not bleed me.' After giving the countess news of George's latest mission to Ireland, she opened her heart to her friend. If we wonder how she could have coped with all she had to bear in life, this letter can help us understand. She wrote:

> *O, dear Madam, what am I and what my father's house that I am so highly favoured to be called a child of God! ... What, to have the great Jehovah, the God of heaven and earth, to be my father, to make my bed in my sickness, to be afflicted in all my affliction; to support me in and under all my trials and temptations and to make his abode with me.*[27]

She did not have a fairy tale marriage, she was childless and unwell, but her focus was on the privilege of being the child of her heavenly Father who loved her, cared for her and understood her.

The Whitefields were married for twenty-seven years. Despite her continuing love for another man, in the early years Elizabeth supported and encouraged her husband in whatever ways she could – writing letters, spurring him to action, travelling with him and running the Bethesda Orphan House in Georgia. Although ill health later prevented her from taking an active part in his ministry, she still travelled to join him when she was able to, and passed on news of her husband's missions to his many supporters. Whitefield described her as his dear yoke fellow, his dear partner and his fellow pilgrim. It may not have been a conventionally happy marriage, but it was a true gospel partnership of respect, support and Christian growth.

Shortly before she died, George wrote: 'My wife is as well as can be expected. Both descending in order to ascend:

> *"Where sin and pain and sorrow cease*
> *and all is calm and joy and peace."'[28]*

Having no news of his wife, a few days later he wrote to a friend from Edinburgh, 'As you do not mention my wife I assume she is out of town.'[29] In fact she was dying.

She died in August 1768. He missed her. He wrote just after she died, 'Sweet bereavements when God himself fills up the chasm! Through mercy I find it so.'[30] A year later he wrote, 'I feel the loss of my right hand daily; but right hands and right eyes must be parted with for Him, who ordereth all things well.'[31] George died two years later. He collapsed while preaching, once again, in his beloved America.

George Whitefield was certainly a better husband than John Wesley, but Elizabeth had many more disappointments in her life than Molly. It would have been natural for her to have become discontented and negative about her marriage and even towards God. She didn't. Through her trust in Christ, she responded supernaturally. She looked to Him and not to her husband to meet her needs, and was able to respond with acceptance, contentment and joy. When she was well enough she used her practical, God-given gifts to support George in his ministry. When she was not, her focus turned increasingly to her eternal future, with eyes fixed on a place where 'sin and pain and sorrow cease and all is calm and joy and peace'. George and Elizabeth, as much as any other couple, had a marriage made in heaven; used for the growth of God's kingdom and their own growth in holiness. If that was true for the Whitefields, it can also be true for any Christian marriage – if knowing Christ and serving Him is at the centre of the relationship.

BIBLE STUDY
& REFLECTION
Philippians 1:27 – 2:4

1. 'Whatever happens, conduct yourselves in a manner worthy of the gospel of Christ.' 1:27. In what different situations did Elizabeth live this out?

2. Which of these situations would you have found the most challenging? Why?

3. How did Elizabeth 'stand firm ... striving together as one for the faith of the gospel without being frightened in any way by those who oppose you' (vv. 27,28)?

4. What were the results of her courage? How can you be more courageous in standing firm for Christ in the face of opposition?

5. In these verses, suffering is shown to be a normal part of the Christian life (vv. 29,30). In what ways did Elizabeth suffer during her life? How did she react?

6. How might understanding that suffering is to be expected (and can even be seen as a privilege, v. 29) help us to react in a more godly way to the difficulties we face in our lives?

7. How far did Elizabeth live out 2:3,4? What impact did her selflessness have on gospel ministry at the time?

8. How might our lives be used for Christ if we looked to the interests of others more often?

CHAPTER FIVE

Sarah Edwards
Worth more than rubies

Reading the description of 'The Wife of Noble Character' in Proverbs 31:10–31 is pretty daunting. She embodies all the qualities outlined in the rest of the book of Proverbs – business sense, hard work, charitableness and hospitality. Her husband and children praise her for her wisdom and godliness. Surely she is too good to be true – an idealized portrait from the ancient world to make the rest of us feel inadequate? Surely this kind of woman couldn't exist in real life – in a world like ours, with real problems and challenges? Or could she? If she could, what would that mean for us? Perhaps we too could aspire to being a walking, talking, epitome of wisdom in our God-given time and place too.

People who met Sarah Edwards reckoned she was this kind of woman. While Elizabeth Whitefield's contemporaries damaged her reputation, the writings of those who met Sarah Edwards had the opposite effect. Visitors such as George Whitefield or Samuel Hopkins, who stayed with the family on and off for two years while being trained for ministry, describe a paragon of Christian womanhood – charming and sophisticated, but godly, disciplined, frugal and kind.

When he first met her as a girl of 13, her future husband, Jonathan Edwards, was overwhelmed by her character and spirituality. Her status as a parenting role model was assured when, in the early 1900s, the pioneering educationalist A.E. Winship, decided to investigate the family tree of Jonathan and Sarah Edwards. Their direct descendants included one U.S. vice-president,[1] three US senators, three governors, three mayors, thirteen college presidents, thirty judges, sixty-five professors, eighty public office holders, 100 lawyers and 100 missionaries.[2]

Sarah lived at the same time as the other women in this book, but in the American colonies, not in Britain. She was born in 1710 in New Haven, Connecticut, only ninety years after the arrival of the Pilgrim Fathers. America was still under direct control of the British, and the towns on the east coast still retained many transatlantic links. British fashion and design were imported or copied and Old World manners and etiquette were still the norm — however inappropriate in a frontier township.

In many ways, the colonies were reliant on Britain — when the New Haven town bell needed repairing it had to be sent 'home' to have the work done. But this Britishness was just a veneer. European settlement was confined to the east coast, and 'Indian country' was only a little way inland. Increasingly, the old families of the first settlers in the New World replaced the English aristocracy as the people of influence. These settlers had often been religious leaders who had led their congregations to America to escape persecution or intolerance in Britain. This meant that church leaders were influential in every community, and moral standards were strictly upheld.

The world of Sarah Edwards was very different from that of her English contemporaries. New Haven had a strictly imposed 9 p.m. curfew. Hogarth would have found no *Gin Lane* in Connecticut.

Sarah was a member of this new aristocracy. Her grandfather, Reverend Thomas Hooker, had fled religious persecution in England in 1633 and settled in Massachusetts. Following a disagreement with the local leaders, he took 100 followers and founded the new colony of Connecticut. Her father, James Pierrepont, was a Congregational minister who had founded not only her hometown of New Haven, but also Yale University. He died when she was just 4 years old, but she had a happy, stable childhood and was brought up in a godly, cultured, educated and relatively wealthy household. She was an attractive and intelligent girl with all the required social graces who had the pick of eligible bachelors.

Jonathan Edwards probably met Sarah when he first arrived at Yale when he was 15 and she was just 8. He only really noticed her when he returned to Yale as a tutor five years later. He was a gangly, intellectual young man, who was not very socially competent. His family was respectable and contained several famous preachers, but it was not in the same league as the Pierreponts. It was also tainted by scandal, as his father's parents had been the first American settlers to get divorced.

Jonathan had been a religious child — whilst other boys would have built a den in the swamp, Jonathan built a prayer hut — but he only became a Christian when he was 19. He was determined to live wholeheartedly for Christ and rise above the lifeless and moralistic religion he saw in many around him. He saw a model of this genuine and joyful Christianity in 13-year-old Sarah. In his famous description of her, he wrote on the flyleaf of a book:

They say there is a young lady in [New Haven] who is beloved of that Great Being, who made and rules the world, and that there are certain seasons in which this Great Being, in some way other or invisible, comes to her and fills her mind with exceeding sweet delight, and that she hardly cares for anything, except to meditate on him — that she expects after a while to be received up where he is, to be raised up out of the world and caught up into heaven; being assured that he loves her too well to let her remain at a distance from him always. There she is to dwell with him, and to be ravished with his love and delight forever. Therefore, if you present all the world before her, with the richest of its treasures, she disregards it and cares not for it, and is unmindful of any pain or affliction. She has a strange sweetness in her mind, and singular purity in her affections; is most just and conscientious in all her conduct; and you could not persuade her to do anything wrong or sinful, if you would give her all the world, lest she should offend this Great Being. She is of a wonderful sweetness, calmness and universal benevolence of mind; especially after this Great God has manifested himself to her mind. She will sometimes go about from place to place, singing sweetly; and seems to be always full of joy and pleasure; and no one knows for what. She loves to be alone, walking in the fields and groves, and seems to have someone invisible always conversing with her.[3]

He doesn't explicitly mention her in his diary again, but over the next few years some have suggested he struggled spiritually, partly due to his obsession with her. A year before their wedding, he wrote, '[It is] just about three years, that I have been for the most part in a low, sunk estate and condition, miserably senseless to what used to be, about spiritual things.'[4] As soon as was respectably possible, when he had become assistant pastor at his grandfather's church in Northampton, and when she was just 17, they got married.

Marrying the minister would have been quite an ordeal for anyone, let alone a teenage girl. Jonathan was seven years older than she was, and had already made a series of resolutions on how to live his life. He worked incredibly hard and had a diet that was so strict that it affected his health. The expectations of the church were daunting. On her first Sunday in church after the wedding, she would have been expected to wear her wedding dress – of green satin brocade – and twirl in front of the congregation of 600 members, so everyone could admire the bride, and the dress. She then had to sit in a raised pew, beneath the pulpit, facing the congregation while her husband preached. This was her seat for the twenty-four years that they spent in

Northampton. As the minister's wife, she would have been one of the most important people in the community, and expected to be an example of morality and piety. Her life was to be lived in the ultimate goldfish bowl. As a mark of respect, the Edwardses were granted the generous salary of $100, a large plot of land and a substantial house near the church. Thankfully, as the daughter of one of the most respected ministers in New Haven, she had been brought up in a similar environment, and even at 17 seemed to relish the role.

From the start, she used her home for hospitality. There was a constant stream of visitors – family and friends, as well as visiting or travelling preachers. In colonial America, the minister's home was expected to function as an inn as much as a family home. Despite living in provincial Northampton, she tried to keep the standards she had been used to in New Haven. The hospitality she offered was far superior to that offered in most homes in the town. The household inventory included luxury items such as a porcelain tea set and damask table cloths, as well as wall mirrors and water colours.[5] Nevertheless, it was not the furnishings but the warmth of the welcome that visitors commented on. Samuel Hopkins, who stayed with the family for some time, commented that Sarah was

educated in the midst of polished life, familiar from childhood with the rules of decorum and good breeding, affable and easy in her manners, and governed by the feelings of liberality and benevolence, she was remarkable for her kindness to her friends, and to the visitants who resorted to Mr Edwards.[6]

This welcome was particularly important, as Jonathan was not very sociable. He aimed to spend thirteen hours a day in his study, and relied on Sarah to deal with all the day-to-day running of the household. He rarely visited parishioners, as he was aware that others could do the job far better, and that he was likely to make people feel uncomfortable. He knew that those who needed him could always find him in his study. His time in the study was not wasted. Apart from helping many with pastoral issues, the sermons and works of theology and philosophy he wrote there are amongst the most profound ever produced.

Jonathan's work meant that Sarah was needed to keep the household functioning as well as to present the human face of the Edwards family to the world. Although Jonathan was said to have had no clue when or if the hay had been gathered in, how many cows he possessed or where the food on his table came from, he wasn't completely useless. Many years later, when they had ten children, Jonathan was left to cope alone when Sarah went to Boston to care for a sick relative, even though several of the children were unwell. After outlining the children's illnesses he went on to write, 'We have been without you almost as long as we know how to be'[7] – a sentiment many modern men would echo in similar circumstances. Jonathan was grateful that it was usually Sarah who ran the home. Samuel Hopkins – perhaps her greatest fan – wrote 'she was the most judicious and faithful mistress of a family, habitually industrious, a sound economist, managing household affairs with diligence and discretion'[8] He doesn't mention that part of the 'managing of household affairs' involved choosing and buying slaves, but once bought they seem to have been treated well.

Jonathan and Sarah were unusual for the time as all eleven of their children survived to adulthood. For the first twenty-two years of her marriage, Sarah gave birth to a child every other year. Each birth was carefully noted in the front page of the family Bible – as well as the date that they had measles. Not surprisingly, much of Sarah's time was spent looking after her eight daughters and three sons. Like Susanna Wesley, her priority was to bring her children up to love and trust the Lord Jesus. Unlike Susanna, she had the wholehearted support of her husband. He wrote, 'Every family ought to be a little church, consecrated to Christ and wholly influenced and governed by His rules. And family education and order are some of the chief means of grace'.[9]

Despite his thirteen hours in the study, he found time to lead family prayers at the start and end of the day, when he would ask each child age-appropriate questions to make sure they had understood the Bible passage that had been read. He also met with the children individually. He saw them in his study to check their spiritual progress, and took them on walks and rides in the country to get to know each of them better. It was still Sarah who did most of the parenting. As Hopkins remarked, 'He could safely commit his children to the wisdom and piety, the love and faithfulness of their mother.'[10] She prayed for her children constantly, even before they were born. She expected respect and good behaviour, and the children always stood when she or Jonathan entered a room. She disciplined them consistently, but never raised her voice. Hopkins was obviously very impressed with the family, but perhaps went a little far when he wrote, 'Quarrelling and contention, which too frequently take place among children, were in her family wholly unknown.'[11]

She wasn't just concerned for the spiritual welfare of her family. She gave encouragement to the many visitors to her home. When Samuel Hopkins was feeling discouraged, it was Sarah who spoke to him and prayed with him. Each evening, before bed, she spent time with Jonathan in his study to pray and discuss theological issues. More controversially at the time, she also organized women's meetings in the parish for prayer and Bible study. Hopkins commented that 'she exerted an important influence over her sex and over the young'.[12]

She was not always viewed so positively in the town. Jonathan's strict moral standards and apparent aloofness made him enemies. When, in 1740, with a growing family, he asked for a pay rise, it was Sarah who took some of the blame for the family's 'extravagance'. The parishioners could not understand why Jonathan needed so many books, nor could they see why Sarah should wear rouge and blue chintz dresses and the children needed to be dressed in Boston fashions rather than simple country clothes. Shortly after the birth of her seventh daughter and the death of her sister, Sarah found the criticism hard to take: she was prone to depression. Jonathan described her as 'subject to unsteadiness and many ups and downs ... often subject to melancholy. She had a disposition to censure and condemn others'.[13] While Jonathan was in his study, Sarah was out and about in the town, and was more aware of the feelings towards her family.

Ironically this was during a time of religious revival in New England. Revival had come to the colonies several times in the past, but had been short-lived. Now, particularly with the arrival of George Whitefield, it was in full flow, and Jonathan was called upon to leave his study and help out by preaching in other towns.

In January 1742, Sarah was feeling particularly low. She wrote, 'I felt very uneasy and unhappy ... I thought I very much needed help from God ... I had for some time been earnestly wrestling with God.'[14] Jonathan was away and they had not parted on good terms. She had criticized a visiting preacher, and Jonathan had told her off. She wrote, 'It seemed to bereave me of the quietness and calm of my mind not to have the good opinion of my husband.'[15] While Jonathan was away, another preacher, Samuel Buell, took his place in the Northampton pulpit. He was a more dynamic speaker, and seemed to be having a greater impact on his listeners than her husband. She struggled with jealousy on his behalf. She could see that God was using Buell and knew that her attitude was wrong. She cried out to God for help, and was able to 'rejoice in the greater success attending his preaching than had followed the preaching of Mr Edwards'.[16]

This was a turning point in her life. She experienced a personal religious awakening. Her 'soul dwelt on high, was lost in God and almost seemed to leave the body'. She had to 'refrain from rising from my seat and leaping for joy'. Over the next few days she had 'a sense of infinite beauty and amiableness of Christ's person, and the heavenly sweetness of his transcendent love'.[17] She was worried what Jonathan would make of her experiences. Unlike the exuberant Whitefield, his preaching had always been very restrained, and for most of his life he read out his sermons from a full script. It seemed unlikely that he would approve of such emotional behaviour. In fact, he was supportive at a time when many were critical of the emotionalism of the revival. He could see that she had become more devoted to Christ, and that she was more and not less able to fulfil all of her household tasks. He asked her to write an account of what had happened to her[18] and used this as the basis of a work of his own, defending the validity of such experiences.[19] He describes her 'constant sweet peace, calm and serenity of soul' and her 'daily sensible doing and suffering everything for God'.[20] Her reputation as a godly woman spread.

One Sunday, Edwards was stuck in snow travelling to preach in another parish. Unable to wait any longer, the young minister of the church began to preach himself, not noticing Edwards arriving at the back of the church. Overcome with embarrassment, he welcomed him profusely, bizarrely ending with the words, 'They say that your wife is going to heaven by a shorter road than yourself.'[21] Jonathan merely nodded and started to preach.

Unfortunately the revival did not end the Edwardses problems with their congregation in Northampton. In fact, the town became increasingly divided between those who had been converted or 'revived', and those who had not. The next few years were difficult. Their financial situation was unstable, and Jonathan was often not paid on time, causing Sarah herself to write to one of the town officials on his behalf, 'I write to desire you to send some as much as you can [sic] as Mr Edwards is under such obligations that he can't possibly do without it.'[22] Resentment towards their expenditure continued, and Jonathan felt obliged to publish an itemized list of the family's outgoings.

It also came to Jonathan's attention that some of the young people of the town were misbehaving. Some boys had got hold of 'bad books' – apparently midwifery handbooks – which at the time were considered virtually pornographic. He named and shamed those responsible from the pulpit. As some of them were from influential Northampton families, the resentment towards him increased. Things got even worse when he decided to tighten up the requirements of those wanting to take Communion. Under his grandfather, anyone had been welcome at the Lord's Supper. Jonathan thought that only established believers should be able to take the bread and wine. Once again resentment mounted. He was accused of having concealed his real views on the matter in order to receive a higher salary.

In 1750, Sarah wrote a lengthy letter in his defence.[23] It was a difficult year. She gave birth to her eleventh child and had rheumatic fever while the church situation worsened. Attendance was down, and eventually 200 members of the congregation signed a petition asking Jonathan to leave.

Jonathan, at 47 years old, with a wife and ten children[24] to support, found himself unemployed. He wrote: 'I am now thrown upon the wide ocean of the world and know not what will become of me and my numerous and chargeable family.'[25] Fortunately, Sarah was adaptable and organized moneymaking ventures for the family so that they did not starve. She and her daughters made lacework, embroidery and painted fans to be sent to market in Boston. Jonathan continued to write, but was now forced to use the margins of pamphlets, envelopes and bits of silk paper left over from making fans. He had little hope of a new parish. He was considered quite old, and because he had been dismissed by the people of Northampton, another church would have been reluctant to take him on.

The following year, the refined and intellectual family made an unlikely move – to the Indian settlement of Stockbridge, Massachusetts. Worshippers were summoned to church by the blast of a conch shell, and most of the Native American congregation were covered in bear fat to keep out the cold. It was not an easy move for Sarah. Life was very different. Her older daughters were getting married, and did not go with them to Stockbridge. There were few visitors to the remote outpost for Sarah to entertain, but she proved to be adaptable once again. She worked with her husband to help and teach the Indian women and children. Jonathan wrote to his elderly father:

> *My wife and children are well pleased with our present situation. They like the place much better than they expected. Here, at present, we live in peace; which has of a long time been an unusual thing with us. The Indians seem much pleased with my family, especially my wife.*[26]

Jonathan made the most of this peaceful situation, and over the next few years wrote some of his most important theological works. He also worked hard in his ministry to the Indians. He tried to simplify his sermons to make life easier for the translator who worked alongside him, and easier for his listeners to understand. Incredibly, he sent his 9-year-old son, Jonathan Jr, off with a missionary to the Indians for an entire year, so that he could learn their language and be equipped for future missionary service.

There may have been relative peace within the church, but conflict was brewing. In 1754, the French and Indian War broke out, and after a number of white settlers were murdered near Stockbridge, the Edwards' home was effectively turned into a fort. For the next three years they were under siege, with four soldiers permanently quartered in their house. Afterwards they submitted a bill to the colonial government for 800 dinners and seven gallons of rum. Their married daughter Esther was reluctant to visit. She wrote, 'I am not so certain about going to Stockbridge for the Indians have made their appearance near Stockbridge, and I don't like to be killed by the barbarian retches.'[27]

Although the war rumbled on, it moved away from Stockbridge, and it looked as though life might return to normal. But it was not to be. Esther's husband, Aaron Burr, had become the president of the newly formed Princeton College, soon to be Princeton University. When he died suddenly, there was a vacancy at the college which the authorities wanted Jonathan to fill. He was reluctant and felt he was unsuitable for the role.

I have a constitution in many respects peculiarly unhappy, attended by flaccid solids, vapid fluids, and a lowtide of spirits; often occasioning a kind of childish weakness and contemptibleness of speech, presence and demeanour, with a disagreeable dullness and stiffness, much unfitting me for conversation, but more especially for the government of a college.[28]

He was nonetheless persuaded to go. Sarah remained in Stockbridge to pack up the house. Before she was able to join him, Jonathan died from complications following a smallpox vaccination. The doctor who had performed the vaccination wrote to tell her the news. She wrote to her daughter Esther:

> *My very dearest child, What shall I say! A holy and good God has covered us with a dark cloud. O that we may kiss the rod and lay our hands on our mouths! The Lord has done it. He has made me adore his goodness, that we have had him so long. But my God lives; and he has my heart. O what a legacy my husband and your father has left us! We are all given to God; and there I am and long to be.*[29]

On the same piece of paper another daughter added, 'My mother wrote this with a great deal of pain in her neck, which disabled her from writing any more.'[30] Esther had also been inoculated, apparently successfully, but sixteen days later she, too, had died of the disease. In the space of a few weeks, Sarah's son-in-law, husband and daughter had died. Although she was unwell, her first instinct was to go to Philadelphia to care for her now orphaned grandchildren. Soon after she arrived, she contracted dysentery and died a few days later — just six months after her husband.

Sarah Edwards was a woman of great faith, but not

without her faults. She was prone to depression, and particularly when younger she could be critical of others, and was accused of extravagance. Her life at times was hard. She had to cope with criticism and hostility towards herself and her husband. She had been used to a settled and prosperous life, but had to face poverty, danger and insecurity after leaving Northampton. She was privileged to lose none of her children when they were young, but then lost her much-loved daughter Jerusha when she was only 18, and later Esther and Aaron Burr and her husband, Jonathan, in a very short time. To us this would seem almost unbearable, but she coped with faith and perseverance.

Her marriage was long and successful, but it cannot always have been easy being married to such an intense and hardworking man. Nevertheless, the descriptions we are given of her by those who met her are of a gracious, godly and gifted woman who generally adapted to the challenges of her life with an unerring trust in God's goodness. She supported her husband through thick and thin, and their marriage has justifiably been seen as a model Christian partnership.

John Walley wrote, 'Surely there is a union of soul among believers, a sensible sweetness at sometimes; I think I love Mr Edwards and his wife, because I see so much of the image of God in them.' Whitefield agreed when he said he had 'never met a sweeter couple'.

John Emerson Concord, after a visit, wrote that the Edwardses were 'the most agreeable family I was ever acquainted with. Much of the presence of God there'.[31]

Perhaps the comment that would have meant most to Sarah was made by her husband on his deathbed, to their daughter Lucy: 'Give my kindest love to my dear wife, and tell her that the uncommon union, which has so long subsisted between us, has been of such a nature, as I trust is spiritual, and therefore will continue for ever.'[32]

He could well have used instead the words from the end of Proverbs 31:

her husband also ... praises her:
'Many women do noble things,
but you surpass them all.'
Charm is deceptive, and beauty is fleeting;
but a woman who fears the LORD is to be praised.[33]

What would our epitaph be?

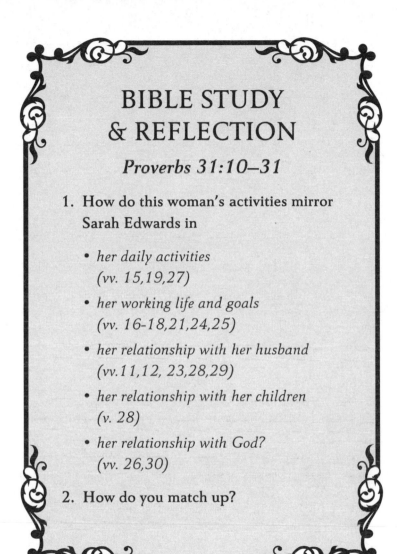

BIBLE STUDY & REFLECTION

Proverbs 31:10–31

1. How do this woman's activities mirror Sarah Edwards in

   - *her daily activities*
     (vv. 15,19,27)

   - *her working life and goals*
     (vv. 16-18,21,24,25)

   - *her relationship with her husband*
     (vv.11,12, 23,28,29)

   - *her relationship with her children*
     (v. 28)

   - *her relationship with God?*
     (vv. 26,30)

2. How do you match up?

CHAPTER SIX

Selina, Countess of Huntingdon
Everything for God

It's tempting to feel virtuous if we respond to the latest charity appeal a little more generously than usual, or if we give up a bit of free time to help out at church. Our culture encourages us to think of our time as precious, and in our busy lives we are taught to make sure we have some 'me time' to relax and indulge ourselves, to prevent stress and burn-out. Shopping can now be 'retail therapy' — spending our hard-earned cash on making ourselves feel better. Surely, within limits, our money and possessions are ours to do with as we please?

Selina, Countess of Huntingdon didn't see her life in that way at all. Once Selina understood the gospel, she was determined to use all of the time, talents and money at her disposal so that as many people as possible could hear the good news for themselves. Selina is the only woman in this book who was well known in her own time. Her position in society, her wealth and her eventual widowhood gave her opportunities not available to most eighteenth century women (or even most twenty-first century women) and, having those opportunities, she used every one.

Selina was born in 1707 in Staunton Harold near Ashby-de-la-Zouch in Leicestershire. Her father was Earl Ferrers, and Staunton Harold was a typical stately home with sweeping lawn, ornamental lake and church attached to the estate. She was born into a world of immense privilege, but even as a child she did not take her life for granted. When she was 9 years old she saw the funeral procession of a child in the village, and after that she often thought about her own death, and would visit the child's grave. She started praying fervently and reading the Bible, and as she grew older she committed herself to living an exemplary life. For a woman of her rank at that time, this was an unusual aim. Normal aristocratic pursuits included gambling, gossiping and flirting, which not infrequently ended in affairs, but Selina had a strong enough character to resist the pressure to conform.

When she was 21 she married 32-year-old Theophilus Hastings, Earl of Huntingdon. It was a great match. He was even wealthier and better connected than she was, but he was also an intelligent, upstanding man, whose family estate at Donington Park was not far from where Selina was brought up. They seem to have genuinely loved each other, and he supported her in her attempts to become the perfect 'Lady Bountiful' – visiting the poor, sick and dying, bringing baskets of food and sharing Bible verses. She wasn't always so conventional. One of her closest friends in London was the outrageous Lady Townshend, who believed it to be her duty to shake up the stuffiness of life at court. Perhaps with her encouragement, Selina wore a series of bizarre dresses, one covered in embroidered lions and snakes, which shocked some of the more fashionable ladies. Selina might have wanted to be good, but she never minded being different.

While Selina was struggling to live a perfect life to win God's approval, her sister-in-law, Margaret Hastings, had had a life-changing experience. She had heard the preaching of Benjamin Ingham, a friend of Whitefield and the Wesleys, and had understood that she could only win God's approval through trusting in Christ's death on the cross on her behalf.[1] She longed for her friends and family to hear the Good News too. One comment she made particularly struck Selina, who remembered her saying 'that since she had known and believed in the Lord Jesus Christ for life and salvation she had been as happy as an angel'.[2]

Soon after, Selina became dangerously ill, and all her old fears of death returned, as she realized that her 'good life' had been anything but good compared to God's perfect standard. She remembered her conversations with Margaret and realized that her only hope was to cast herself on God's mercy and to trust in Christ alone. The effect was immediate and dramatic. She was overwhelmed with a feeling of joy and peace, and her fear of death disappeared.

Like Margaret, her first instinct was to share her new faith with family and friends. She immediately invited the Wesley brothers, who were in the area, to preach at Donington Park. Friends in her social circle were horrified and even suggested that she was showing signs of family madness, already displaying itself in the bizarre behaviour of her cousin, the new Earl Ferrers. Some advised her husband to exert his authority and stamp out Selina's religious enthusiasm. He didn't. Although he never became a Christian, he always supported her, and accompanied her to hear preachers at Donington and also in London. He commented to one visiting preacher, 'The morality of the Bible I admire, but the Atonement I cannot comprehend.'[3]

From the start, Selina was determined to use her social position to share the gospel with the aristocracy. Not all responded positively. This was the Duchess of Buckingham's reply to one invitation:

> *I thank your Ladyship for the information concerning the Methodist preaching; these doctrines are most repulsive and strongly tinctured with impertinence and disrespect towards their superiors in perpetually endeavouring to level all ranks and do away with all distinctions, as it is monstrous to be told that you have a heart that is as sinful as the common wretches that crawl on the earth. This is highly offensive and insulting; and I cannot but wonder that your Ladyship should relish any sentiment so much at variance with high rank and good breeding.*[4]

Selina wasn't put off. Although many others were also appalled by the democratic nature of the gospel, some were intrigued. Sarah, Duchess of Marlborough wrote:

> *My dear Lady Huntingdon is also so very good to me, and I really do feel so very sensibly all your kindness and attention, that I must accept your very obliging invitation to accompany you to hear Mr Whitefield, though I am still suffering from the effects of a severe cold. Your concern for my improvement and religious knowledge is very obliging and I do hope that I shall be the better for your excellent advice.*[5]

A few accepted Christ for themselves, including her friends Colonel and Lady Frances Gardiner. Her aunt, Lady Fanny Shirley, also became a Christian and, following her niece's example, turned her famous literary salon into a venue for Methodist meetings.

Selina did not confine herself to sharing the gospel with her wealthy friends; she reached out to everybody she came into contact with. When preachers came, services were also held for the servants, so that they too could hear the Good News. When she visited the poor on the estate, she took the opportunity to talk about Jesus as well as to bring the expected basket of food. She spoke with the estate workers when she could. She once spoke to a labourer at work on the garden wall about eternal things. Some time later she was talking to another workman and said,

'Thomas, I fear you never pray, or look to Christ for salvation.' 'Your Ladyship is mistaken,' replied the man; 'I heard what passed between you and James at the garden wall, and the word you meant for him took effect on me.' 'How did you hear it?' she asked. 'I heard it,' Thomas answered, 'on the other side of the garden, through a hole in the wall, and I shall never forget the impression I received.'[6]

Throughout her life she continued to speak to the poor as well as the wealthy. Years later, while she was staying in Brighton, hoping that the sea air and 'taking the waters' would cure her dying son, she visited a destitute sailor's wife. She brought food and took the opportunity to explain the gospel. The woman's home shared a very thin wall with a bakehouse, where the poor brought their food to be cooked. Gradually the customers at the bakehouse started listening in to the conversations next door. One listener was a blacksmith called Joseph Wall, who was infamous in Brighton for his drunkenness and violent behaviour. Wanting to hear more, he left the bakehouse and crept into a corner of the room where Selina was speaking. He understood the message and was transformed. For the remaining twenty-nine years of his life, he was famous in Brighton for his gentleness and godliness.

For ten years after her conversion, Selina did what she could. She was limited, despite the support of her husband, by the conventions that surrounded her position of dutiful wife and mother and society hostess. She had seven children, six surviving infancy. In 1744, two of her beloved sons, George, who was 14, and Ferdinando who was 11, both died of smallpox. Two years later her husband was also dead, at the age of just 50. She was only 39.

Shortly after his death, she wrote to Dodderidge, one of 'her ministers':

I hope you will never care about the ceremony of time in your letters to me, but just when attended with greatest ease to yourself, for we both agree that the one thing worth living for must be proclaiming the love of God to man in Christ Jesus as for me, I want no holiness he does not give me; I can wish for no liberty but what he likes for me, and I am satisfied with every misery he does not redeem me from, that in all things I may feel, 'without him I can do nothing.'[7]

Although she was already one of the key supporters of the new Methodist movement – shortly after her sons' deaths she hosted the very first Methodist conference at her home in London – after her husband's death she became more and more involved. After a period of mourning in Bath, rather than setting off for the customary recuperative tour of the European spas, Selina organized a preaching tour of Wales. Selina, her daughters and sisters-in-law, Lady Anne and Lady Frances Hastings, accompanied by Howell Harris and others, travelled from village to village, holding gospel meetings. According to Lady Frances Hastings, 'The divine influence of the spirit of God was very evidently afforded with his word, and many were added to His number.'[8]

As a widow, Selina was able to use her position without the restraining influence of her husband. She complained to parliament when she learned that Welsh magistrates were harassing preachers. Later she even complained to the king about the disreputable parties that the Archbishop of Canterbury was holding in his palace! Such was her status in society and the strength of her personality that she was taken seriously. The magistrates were humiliated by having to pay back the money they had extorted from the preachers, and the Archbishop was told off by the King. George III was always sympathetic towards Selina and the gospel, but her views didn't go down well with the rest of the royal family. Horace Walpole snidely commented, 'The queen of the Methodists got her daughter named for lady of the bed chamber to the princesses; but it is all off again, as she will not let her play cards on Sunday.'[9]

Although she had always invited men such as the Wesleys and Whitefield to her home to preach, her house now became a refuge for exhausted itinerant preachers. Whitefield enjoyed the rest at Ashby, one of the countess's country homes: 'And Ashby-Place is like a Bethel, we have the sacrament every morning, heavenly conversation all day, and preaching at night. This is "to live at court indeed."'[10] The locals were not enthusiastic, and rioting accompanied the preaching. Whitefield wrote to a friend:

> *Good Lady Huntington is weak in body, but strong in grace. Thousands and thousands flock to hear the word twice every day, and the power of God has attended it in a glorious manner. But the good people of Ashby were so kind as to mob round her Ladyship's door while the gospel was preached. Ashby is not worthy of so rich a pearl.*[11]

In 1748, she appointed Whitefield her personal chaplain, which gave him more freedom to preach outside of Anglican pulpits. As a member of the aristocracy, she had the right to appoint a personal chaplain on her own terms. As it became harder for evangelical preachers to be accepted by the Church of England authorities, she appointed more and more chaplains. With preachers often barred from pulpits, she set about building chapels so that the gospel could be proclaimed and the congregations built up. By the time of her death she had founded sixty-three chapels. She funded the building work personally, and even sold £3,700-worth of jewels to finance the building of the new chapel in Brighton. The chapels were to be for all classes of society, but she hoped that those built in the fashionable towns of Brighton, Bath and Tunbridge

Wells would give her upper-class friends a chance to hear the Good News. In her chapel in Bath, there was even a 'Nicodemus' corner' where the nobility, and even bishops, could sit behind a curtain and hear the preaching without being spotted.

Many of her preachers were ordained members of the Church of England with their own parishes, but as access to training and ordination became more difficult for evangelicals, she decided it was time to set up her own college to train godly men for ministry. In 1767 she founded Trevecca College in Wales. Once again she covered all the costs personally. She also took a careful interest in the details of the college and the students. According to one student, each one was given 'lodging, diet, clothing, a horse, gown, cassock, bands and a small amount of money'[12] He particularly treasured his initialled handkerchief! Her interest in the students carried on even after they left. She wrote lengthy and personal letters about their clothes and health, as well as detailed plans for preaching tours, and other opportunities for ministry. Her chapels and preachers formed an informal 'connexion' within the Church of England. She saw that the doctrines of the established church were perfectly compatible with a biblical, gospel ministry, and she expected her preachers to stand by the Anglican Thirty-Nine articles and to use only the Book of Common Prayer.

She was less prepared to stand by those she disagreed with within the Methodist movement. Selina favoured Whitefield's more Calvinistic theology over Wesley's Arminian views,[13] but until Whitefield's death in 1770 she had worked hard to help the two men overcome their differences. However, when the minutes of the Wesleyan Methodists' conference in 1770 appeared to be directly opposed to Calvinist doctrine, Selina saw red. She insisted that every member of her college must refute Wesley's ideas or leave. Having worked together for the gospel for many years, both the headmaster and the president of the college refused to denounce the Wesleyans and were forced to resign. Although eventually both sides saw that the differences had been overstated, the damage was done, as supporters of each group wrote increasingly unpleasant pamphlets to discredit the other side.

Augustus Toplady, writer of 'Rock of Ages' wrote a particularly offensive tract on behalf of the Calvinists, which spoiled both their and his reputation. John Wesley typically refused to see that there had been any fault on his side. Selina — ever the aristocrat — was even more firmly convinced that she was right. Although the Revolution in America soon diverted attention from the controversy, the breach was final. Selina remained friendly with Charles and Sally Wesley, but she never worked alongside John and the Wesleyans again. Her forceful and energetic personality, which had proved so valuable in establishing and supporting her college and chapels was, on this occasion, a force for harm, not good.

Having separated from the Wesleyans, it was not long before her 'connexion' also had to separate from the Church of England. In 1776, a large theatre, the Pantheon, came up for sale in Clerkenwell, London, which Selina thought would be ideal as a chapel. She wrote:

> *My heart seems strangely set upon having this temple of folly dedicated to Jehovah Jesus ... I feel so deeply for the perishing thousands in that part of London, that I am almost tempted to run every risk; and though at this moment I have not a penny to command, yet I am so firmly persuaded of the goodness of the Master whose I am, and whom I desire to serve, that I shall not want for gold nor silver for the work.[14]*

She raised the money from supporters and bought the building. It was immediately put to good use, even before it was properly converted. An early visitor described the scene: 'A pulpit was erected on the stage ... people used to go into the boxes, pit and gallery ...whenever anything was spoken ... which the people approved ... they immediately clapped hands for a short time as at a play!'[15] She soon set about changing the Pantheon theatre properly into the Spa Fields Chapel, and installing her own preachers. She appointed Charles Wesley's son as music director at the chapel as a favour to her old friend.

By this time she had many chapels served by her own chaplains, which she believed was within her rights as a member of the aristocracy. That right was challenged by the vicar of the parish in which the new chapel was found. As vicar, he said he, and he alone, had the right to preach in the parish. He took the countess to court and won. Her only options were to close her chapels or leave the Church of England and for her 'connexion' to become a new denomination, which would allow her chapels to continue under the Toleration Act. She had no choice but to leave. It was a hollow victory for the vicar. The Spa Fields Chapel became the headquarters of the new movement in London, and the gospel continued to be preached there by a succession of Trevecca-trained ministers. It was also the setting for the first ordinations in the new denomination in 1783. The Countess of Huntingdon's Connexion was born.

She had been working tirelessly for the gospel for over forty years. Her influence spread throughout Britain, through her chapels, preachers and also her aristocratic contacts. King George III was a fan. When a bishop complained about her, the King remarked, 'I wish there was a Lady Huntingdon in every diocese in the

Kingdom.'[16] Indirectly, her influence also spread to America, which she had become interested in through Whitefield.[17] Missionaries were sent from Trevecca to work with the American Indians. They were asked at their commissioning service, 'Who will go for us? Who will publish the glad tidings of great good in the forests and frontiers of the world?'[18] She was anxious to go herself, but never made it: 'I can not help thinking that the Lord will have me there before I die; if only to make coats and garments for the poor Indians.'[19]

She personally sponsored the writing of the first African-American female poet, Phyllis Wheately. Despite owning slaves herself in America, she also supported the abolitionist and freed slave Olaudah Equiano, who in turn supported her recently formed London Missionary Society. The sponsorship of a member of the nobility meant their writings reached a far wider audience than would otherwise have been the case. She was anxious to reach out to everyone with the gospel, and to support Christian men and women from whatever background or race.

Her international reputation and her willingness to make the most of every opportunity nearly led to disaster. Lord Douglas was a committed Roman Catholic who lived in Brussels. He knew of the impact the Methodists were having in Britain, and was determined to put a stop to it. He believed that the death of the Countess of Huntingdon would do irreparable damage to the Methodist movement, and planned to assassinate her!

The plot was years in the planning. In the mid-1770s he had come to London and feigned conversion to Methodism to win her trust. When in 1786 he appealed to Selina to come to Brussels to bring the gospel to the Belgians she responded immediately, even though she was nearly 80 at the time. She wrote to a friend as she set off, 'Sickness and business daily almost overpower my old age.' Nevertheless she had 'a large chapel taken for me at Brussels',[20] and even planned to travel from there to Germany. She was delayed on the way to London, and by the time she arrived, a series of letters outlining the plot had been discovered. She later found out that Lord Douglas had dropped dead suddenly on the day that she had set off for the continent!

It was not just 'sickness and business' that overpowered her old age. Apart from her husband and two sons who had died so young, Selina had also lost another son, Henry, when he was just 18 and her daughter Selina, who had been a committed Christian and great support to her mother, had died aged 26 in 1763. Her daughter Elizabeth was living in Ireland, having married the Earl of Moira. Only her eldest son, Francis, now the Earl of Huntingdon, was around to support her. Unfortunately he was not much help, and never understood her rather embarrassing commitment to the unfashionable cause of the gospel, and so was never given much help. He even failed in an earl's main priority, by only managing to produce an illegitimate heir.

One by one her close friends died. Many died as Christians, often because of her witness. Others did not. Her close friend Lord Chesterfield had raised her hopes many times when he had accompanied her to hear one of 'her preachers', but he refused even to see a minister on his deathbed. Selina visited a few days before he died and wrote, 'The blackness accompanied by every gloomy horror thickened most awfully around his dying moments.'[21] Eventually, two years before Selina, her son Francis died. Apparently he was willing to have a preacher with him, but Selina does not seem to have believed that he turned to Christ at the last moment.

Despite 'sickness and business' and the inevitable loneliness of outliving almost all her friends and family, Selina had a productive and contented old age. She lived in a simple apartment next to the Spa Fields Chapel with her friend and companion Lady Anne Irskine. By now she had almost no money of her own, having used it all to fund gospel work, but she always kept £300 to pay for her funeral – in particular to pay for a white satin dress to be buried in. When she heard that the Birmingham chapel needed £300, she was reluctant to give it until Lady Anne told her off for her lack of faith: 'You can trust God with your soul; why not with your funeral?'[22] The day that the money was sent to Birmingham, a cheque for £300 arrived in the post addressed to the countess. God could be trusted with her funeral – and with providing her with a faithful and straight-talking friend.

She was so generous that her friends tended not to tell her when they were in financial difficulty, knowing that she would go without herself in order to help. One visitor at this stage of her life was overwhelmed by her simple lifestyle.

> *What a lesson! Can a person of her noble birth, nursed in the lap of grandeur, live in such a house, so meanly furnished? And shall I a tradesman be surrounded with luxury and elegance? From this moment I shall hate my house, my furniture, and myself for spending so little for God and so much in folly.*[23]

Towards the end of her life, Selina only allowed herself one new dress a year – like the poorer members of her Spa Fields congregation. Everything she received she gave to support gospel work. After her death, a friend wrote:

> *Never perhaps did mortal make nobler use of what she possessed, live less attached to the earth*

and its unrighteous Mammon, or dispense it with a more open hand. She was one of the poor who lived upon her own bounty. If she grudged anything it was to herself. Never did human being sit so loose to money, or more jealously watch over the distribution of it, that every shilling she possessed should be employed to the glory of God.[24]

She was also determined that every moment of her time should be well spent. She was very ill for the last months of her life, but just days before she died she was planning sending missionaries to Otaheile, now known as Tahiti, in the south Pacific. She knew too that if her life's work was not to crumble when she died, she needed to plan for the future. She set up a trust with Lady Anne in charge, and wrote a will leaving her chapels (and debts) to the trust with instructions on how the work should continue. Up until then, she had paid close attention to every detail of the work. It was her energy and vision that started and maintained everything, from the chapels and the college at Trevecca to missionary work and financial and pastoral support for individual preachers. That the Countess's 'Connexion' survived into the twentieth century shows that her forward planning succeeded, and that her trust in Lady Anne Irskine was well founded.

In her last few months she became increasingly frail, but for such an active and energetic woman she does not seem to have become frustrated. She was 84 and, after a long and active life, looked forward to 'going home'. Shortly before she died, she said, 'My work is done; I have nothing to do but to go to my Father.'[25] In worldly terms, she was a peeress from one of the greatest families in England: in spiritual terms, she was one of the most influential people of her generation — but to the end she saw herself as just another forgiven sinner on a par with the thief on the cross. She said to a visiting friend a few days before her death, 'I see myself a poor worm ... I confess my dear friend, I have no hope but that which inspired the dying malefactor at the side of my Lord; and I must be saved in the same way, as freely, as fully, or not at all.'[26] She finally 'went home' in June 1791, just three months after John Wesley.

Her understanding of the enormous generosity of God in sending His Son to die in her place led to her extraordinary generosity and sacrifice in return. She knew that all her earthly wealth, status and comfort were nothing compared to what she had in Christ. In fact, she was aware that as a noblewoman she was particularly privileged to have been accepted by God. She said, 'O bless the Lord for the letter "M" in 1Corinthians 1:26 that it is not said not any, but not many noble called; and especially bless Him, that through grace my soul is among the number of the highly favoured few.'[27] She was prepared to give up all the privileges of her birth so that others could hear the Good News of the gospel, as she had. She didn't give up all her aristocratic qualities. She had an inbuilt confidence from her background which meant she felt at home in palaces and hovels, but she also felt she had a right to organize and direct her chapels and preachers, which to some seemed dictatorial. She could be impatient with those who did not have her energy or commitment, and was used to having commands obeyed. Despite these failings she was seen then, and since, as a godly and gracious woman, who played an unparalleled role in the spread of the gospel. Even the Roman Catholic John Henry Newman, who objected to her evangelical beliefs, wrote:

> *She devoted herself, her name, her means, her time, her thoughts, to the cause of Christ. She did not spend her money on herself; she did not allow the homage paid to her rank to remain with herself: she passed these on, and offered them up to Him from whom her gifts came ... She was the representative, in an evil day, of what was, then as now, lost to the Church, — of the rich becoming poor for Christ, of delicate women putting off their soft attire and wrapping themselves in sack-cloth for the kingdom of heaven's sake.[28]*

BIBLE STUDY & REFLECTION

Philippians 3:4b–11

1. What reasons did Selina have to 'put confidence in the flesh' (i.e. trust in what she had naturally rather than spiritually) vv. 4–6? What reasons might you have?

2. In what ways did Selina show that she considered all these things ' a loss compared to the surpassing worth of knowing Christ Jesus my Lord' (v. 8) in her attitude to

   • *her material possessions*
   • *her friends and family?*
   • *God's people?*

3. How has 'the surpassing worth of knowing Christ Jesus my Lord' changed your attitude to these things?

4. How far did Selina's priorities and purpose in life match those shown in verses 8–11?

5. How has your commitment to Christ changed your priorities and purpose in life?

CHAPTER SEVEN

Mary Newton
Just ordinary?

Selina, Countess of Huntingdon was extraordinary. She had status, wealth and God-given gifts that she used in His service. Most of us are just plain ordinary – of average looks, intelligence and talent. Looking at Selina's life could leave us feeling extremely inadequate. The great news is that God can use each one of us, however ordinary we may be. Mary Newton, the wife of John, the writer of 'Amazing Grace', was in many ways a very ordinary woman. A young friend of her husband's commented, 'Mr Newton's attachment to his wife was extreme. Some have wondered at this as she seemed to them to have few, if any attractions.'[1]

She was not particularly well educated, her health was poor, and spiritually she seems to have been quite a slow learner. However, God used this ordinary woman in some extraordinary ways.

John Newton always credited Mary with playing a key role in his conversion — well before she became a Christian herself. He first met Mary Catlett when he was 17 and she was just 13. Their mothers were cousins and close friends, but John's mother had died when he was only 6, and after his father's remarriage the families had drifted apart. His mother had been a keen Christian, but his father was not and John's new stepmother fitted the fairy tale stereotype. When she had a child of her own, John was packed off to boarding school for two years, until he was old enough, at 10, to go to sea with his father, who was captain of a ship.

For the first few years, John was protected on board by his father, but he became increasingly rebellious and his father was not convinced that John was suited to a career at sea. A friend had contacts in Jamaica, where there was a job for John managing a sugar plantation. He was all set to go, when out of the blue he got a letter from the Catletts asking him to stay at their home in Chatham, Kent. As he had to go to Kent on some business for his father, he called in. He had planned to stay a few days en route, but he ended up staying for three weeks, missing the boat to Jamaica, and so changing the course of his life. John had fallen in love with Mary, although she was totally unaware of the fact. Years later, John wrote:

> *Almost at the first sight of this girl, for she was then under fourteen, I was impressed with an affection for her which never abated or lost its influence a single moment in my heart from that hour. In degree it actually equalled all that the writers of romance have imagined. In duration it was unalterable.[2]*

Having missed the boat to Jamaica, John was stuck with a life at sea. First in the Mediterranean and then the Atlantic, his lifestyle was that of an archetypical sailor — or even worse. He was known for his bad language and bad attitude, and was often disciplined for insubordination. His life appeared to be out of control, but there was one fixed point — his love for Mary.

> *When I afterwards made shipwreck of faith, hope and conscience, my love to this person was the only remaining principle, which in any degree supplied their place, and the bare possibility of seeing her again was the only present and obvious means of restraining me from the most horrid designs against myself and others.[3]*

He took every opportunity to spend time with her when he was back in England, even if that meant being absent without leave. On one occasion he was caught, imprisoned, whipped and demoted from his position as midshipman for leaving his ship without permission. Back on board, he dreamed of murdering the captain, but his love for Mary stopped him. He later wrote:

> *In a word my love for Mrs N was now the only restraint I had left. Though I neither feared God nor regarded men, I could not bear that she should think meanly of me when I was dead ... This single thought ... proved my only and effectual barrier against the greatest and most fatal temptations.*[4]

When the hated captain died, John must have hoped that life would get better, but the new captain treated him even worse. Hoping to improve his situation, John asked to be left at an African slave-trading station in the Plantanes to work with a European trader. The situation sounds idyllic: 'A low sandy island, about two miles in circumference and almost covered in palm trees.'[5] His life there was anything but. Being unwell, he was unable to travel with the trader, and was left behind with his boss's African 'wife' who took every opportunity to mistreat him. He was beaten, shackled and starved – his only comfort was a book of Euclidean mathematics, which he studied from cover to cover.

Even when he was able to go on a slaving trip inland with his master, he was maliciously accused of theft. It was the rainy season and he was forced to live on the deck of the river boat, with no shelter and few clothes. His health never fully recovered. He was giving up hope of ever seeing Mary again, and his prospects were so poor that he knew he would never be able to marry her.

John had lost contact with his family at home, but his father had never stopped searching for him, and asked a sea captain friend to look for his son on a trip to West Africa. By an extraordinary coincidence he found him, but John was reluctant to return to England. He now had a better boss, and assuming he could never marry Mary, he was willing to take his chances and try to make his fortune as a slave trader. It was only when the captain, untruthfully, told him that there was a large legacy waiting for him at home, which would make him an eligible match, that he agreed to leave. It was his love for Mary, once again, that changed the course of his life.

His behaviour did not change. On his new ship he was told off for blaspheming by the captain, and nearly drowned following a drinking competition. In quieter moments he still studied mathematics and read a copy of Stanhope's edition of Thomas à Kempis's *Life of Christ*, which he found on board. Then a storm struck. Soon the ship started to sink and only the cargo of bees wax and wood kept it afloat. The crew tied themselves to the ship with ropes to stop them being washed away. John was sure he was about to die. He wrote, 'I thought if the Christian religion was true I could not be forgiven.'[6] He worked for nine hours at the pump, slept for an hour and then was at the helm for another eleven hours.

John decided to pray, and miraculously the hard work began to pay off. Over the next two weeks, as the ship struggled against strong winds and the crew faced starvation, he started to read the Bible. When they finally reached port in the north of Ireland, John knew that God had heard and answered his prayers. He was determined to live a new life. He gave up swearing and attended church twice every day. He also now knew that he had been lied to about the legacy. He was a poor man and gave up any thoughts of marriage.

Unknown to him, his father and Mary's family had other plans. Somehow they had agreed to the match while he was away. As soon as he saw that he had a chance, he travelled to Kent to propose. It did not go well. A couple of years later, he reminded Mary of what had happened. After refusing him a couple of times '

> you heard me without interrupting me, and from thence proceeded to argue and object, in a cool conversible strain. When it came to this, I promised myself success. I remembered that line 'The woman that deliberates is gain'd.' I then began to press my

point more closely, till you actually yielded, and gave me your hand in consent.[7]

Mary's reluctance is understandable. She was agreeing to marry a sailor who would be at sea for most of the year, and a man who seemed incapable of keeping out of trouble. She would have been surprised to learn that she was agreeing to marry a new, but increasingly enthusiastic Christian, who would soon be known not as a hellraiser but as a pastor and preacher.

John soon had to go away to sea again. He struggled to live as a Christian at sea, but began to study the Bible and improve his Latin, while rounding up, transporting and selling slaves. On his return, John and Mary were married. He was 25, she was 21. John later wrote, 'At that time we knew not God'.[8] John was a baby Christian, but Mary was no more than a Sunday churchgoer – Newton wrote:

> *She was not wanting in that decent religion which is compatible with the supposed innocent gaieties of a worldly life, which disposes people to be equally ready and punctual (in their respective seasons) at church and at cards – at the assembly or the theatre, and at the sacrament. Farther than this she knew not.*[9]

They were together for three months before John was offered the captaincy of his own slave ship. Already he realized that although his love for Mary had prevented him from getting into serious trouble earlier on, it now threatened to draw him away from love for God, and to become 'an idolatrous attachment. Their time apart was to benefit them both.

For the first five years of their marriage, Mary lived with her family in Kent while John captained his slave ship. They were only together for about a month each year, and each time he went to sea she knew he might not return. Her family and friends were not Christians, and she lived a comfortable, sociable and conventional life. Their separation could have been disastrous for their marriage, if it had not been for John's frequent letters. He expressed himself in writing far better than face to face. He admitted that the letters might not have been what she expected. 'Were some gay ladies of your acquaintance to read what I write, they would call much of it, stuff, and preaching; and admire that you have patience to read it.'[10]

Mary must have been pleasantly surprised, but also confused by the change in her new husband. His letters were full of his love for her, but also his hopes that she would share his faith. He wrote in another letter: 'My prayers for you are, for your health, peace and satisfaction, while we are separated, and for our happy meeting; but above all, for your progress in religion, and that you may have a prospect of happiness, independent of all earthly comforts; and superior to them.'[11] She did ask him to write less serious letters, but she still read each one carefully and, as John wrote later, 'in due time God was pleased to make them a means of affecting her heart, and impressing her with the same desires and aims'.[12] Her letters clearly showed her spiritual progress. John wrote, 'Were I master of the whole coast of Africa, I would part with it, to procure you the same ground, and degree of peace, which I possess myself; and am willing to hope you are, by this time, not far, if at all behind me.'[13]

Only two years into their marriage she was the one that suggested that they should pray together. John wrote, 'I was ... greatly hindered by a cowardly reserved spirit; I was afraid of being thought precise; and though I could not live without prayer, I durst not propose it even to my wife, till she herself first put me upon it.'[14] John's letters changed Mary, but they also changed him. Realizing that what he wrote could be of eternal significance encouraged John to begin a lifelong ministry of letter writing, which he believed had more spiritual impact than all his other activities.

We all have expectations of how our lives will turn out. How we react when these expectations are not met says a lot about our character. Mary expected her life to continue in Kent, with her family and friends around her, coping with a growing family of her own, while John's seafaring career flourished. She was wrong. John and Mary never had children of their own, and John's career was cut short when, while on leave, he suddenly had an unexpected seizure. It seemed to be an epileptic fit, and he was declared medically unfit to go to sea. The shock of John's illness and possible death led to Mary becoming seriously ill herself. John never had another fit, but Mary's health was always delicate after this.

John needed to find a job on land fast, partly to pay their medical bills. The role of Surveyor of Tides came up in Liverpool, and John was recommended for the job. He had to move there alone as Mary was too ill to travel. Unwell and unsettled by the sudden change in her life, Mary was determined to build her life on Christ's solid rock. The letters John wrote during this time show that he was delighted by Mary's growing spiritual maturity. 'It makes my heart glad to see in you one mark of a real believer, in that you love the ministers and people of the Lord and are not offended with the gospel.'[15] She wrote to him about the sermons she had heard, and John's new friend George Whitefield was impressed by her when he met her in London. 'I have several times had the pleasure of conversing with Mrs N. God has been pleased to give her a great measure of your spirit. She is neither afraid nor ashamed to own her profession.'[16]

That Mary was 'neither afraid nor ashamed' to be known as a committed Christian was not without cost. Her family disapproved of religious 'enthusiasm', and in particular the fact that Christians of all backgrounds socialized together. John wrote to reassure Mary that when she moved to Liverpool 'I am far from proposing that you shall keep company with washerwomen', as her aunt had suggested might happen, but Mary was already making friends with Christians of all classes. John continued, 'I perceive that you likewise have picked a fine set of methodistical acquaintances. Should your aunt know it, she would set you down as almost ruined.'[17]

John looked forward to being able to establish their own Christian home, unlike Mary's socially acceptable but ungodly home in Kent: 'Such a house as it will be our duty and privilege to keep; where God may be worshipped, and nothing practised or permitted that is contrary to our Christian profession.'[18] Mary was willing to risk her family's disapproval in order to put Christ, rather than convention, at the centre of her new life with John. John had always been devoted to Mary; that she was now devoted to Christ meant that she could be a spiritual as well as an emotional support for her husband.

The move to Liverpool was the first of several changes that Mary had to adapt to. John's work in Liverpool was quite easy, and he had plenty of spare time to study theology and to get involved in church life. Within a few years he felt called to full-time ministry and had made his first – unsuccessful – attempts at preaching. He was uncertain which road to take. He had Baptist, Independent, Methodist and Anglican friends, and felt equally at home in each circle. After some false starts it appears to have been Mary who encouraged him to consider ordination in the Church of England. Early on in the process he gained her family's approval, which would have been unlikely if he had chosen to become a nonconformist minister. 'Our family are all well and well pleased with my design; although some of them express a little of their cares, and fears about money matters.'[19]

John did not have a university degree – then a requirement for Anglican ordination – and he was also known for his evangelical views. Acceptance by the authorities proved to be a long and drawn-out process. Although ordination would mean a significant drop in income, Mary was a constant source of support: 'You have from the first rise of this affair, acted a part, which perhaps few of your sex could equal. To make such sacrifices, so cheerfully and upon such slender grounds is not common. I can only say it has not been lost on me.'[20] 'I have no one to whom I can unbosom myself; or if I had a thousand friends, they would signify little without you.'[21] Without Mary's support, John Newton would never have entered the ministry.

Eventually, John was appointed minister of the Parish of Olney in Northamptonshire. It was very unlike the world that Mary had grown up in, or even their life in Liverpool. Olney was a poor community and the Newtons were the only family to have servants. Mary got as involved in the parish as her health would allow, and her work was appreciated. While she was away, John wrote urging her to come home soon: 'I speak not merely upon my own account; you are greatly wanted by the sick, by the poor and by your family.'[22] Even when she was not well, her very presence encouraged and helped John. He wrote:

> *I can do more business in two days when you are at home, than in three when you are abroad. For though I sit many an hour in my study, without seeing you, yet to know that you are in, or about the house, and that I can see you when I please gives a sort of composure to my mind.*[23]

John's ministry flourished and his fame grew, particularly when the story of his conversion became a runaway bestseller. Mary supported him in the background, entertaining the many guests to the vicarage, providing a listening ear and a calming presence for her dynamic and sometimes volatile husband.

It was not just John whose ministry benefited from

her kindness and hospitality. William Cowper was a committed Christian and brilliant poet, but suffered from severe depression. He moved to Olney to be near Newton. He lived in the Newtons' home for five weeks while his own house was being renovated, and later for thirteen months after a suicide attempt. During this time he was mentally unstable and needed constant care. Cowper's aunt wrote to thank the Newtons: 'Nor can I be insensible of what you yourself, Mrs Newton ... must suffer in your attention to him, may every comfort you are enabled to give be returned in multiplied blessings to your own souls.'[24] Cowper's friendship with the Newtons almost certainly saved his life, but also gave him opportunities for parish visiting, at which he was very gifted, and for collaborating with John on the *Olney Hymns*, a collection which included John's 'Amazing Grace'. Without Mary's support for both men, it is possible that one of the world's best-loved hymns would never have been written.

Mary did not have her own children, but she had God-given opportunities to use her gifts to care for other members of her family. She looked after her elderly father in Kent, which meant being away from home for ten weeks as heavy snow stopped her travelling back with him to Olney. He died six months later, with his daughter by his side. Mary and John also rejoiced in the opportunity to adopt Mary's orphaned nieces – first 5-year-old Betsy, and later the teenaged Eliza.

For a middle-aged couple, even without Mary's poor health, this would have been a challenge, but they both rose to the occasion. John wrote to Mary shortly after Betsy arrived, 'Give my love to my dear child who, I hope and believe, will be a good girl. And I beg of her and all who are about her, that your rules, to which she so cheerfully submits when at home, may be broken as little as possible.'[25] Eliza came to live with them after they had left Olney and moved to London. Her parents had both died of tuberculosis and she already had the disease. Mary took her to stay in Southampton, hoping that a 'sea cure' might help.[26] It didn't, and Eliza died soon after. She was a remarkably godly child, and both John and Mary were encouraged and challenged by her faith in the face of suffering. Mary adored Eliza. John wrote:

> Eliza well knew [Mary's] feelings; and a concern for her was, I believe, the last anxiety that remained with her. She said to those about her 'Try to persuade my aunt to leave the room; I think I shall soon go to sleep. I shall not remain with you till the morning.' Her aunt however was the last person who heard her speak, and was sitting by her bed when she went away.[27]

Their other adopted daughter, Betsy, learned from her aunt's example of caring for the wider family, and after

Mary's death looked after John in his old age.

Mary's life changed again when in 1780 the Newtons moved to the parish of St Mary's Woolnoth in London. Their final years in Olney had not gone well. Numbers were down at church services and prayer meetings, and John described the younger people in the town as 'sermon proof'. Other churches begged the famous John Newton to lead them. St Mary's attracted a far wider circle of people than the poor farmers in Olney. John described his new congregation: 'My church is full and crowded ... there are many eminent Christians among them ... and we have particularly a fine show of young people springing up and increasing in numbers and graces, like willows by the water courses.'[28]

In many ways, it was a happy time. John was one of very few evangelical Anglican ministers in London, and his preaching attracted huge crowds. He became friends with the young William Wilberforce, who he encouraged to remain in politics, and with the intellectual Hannah More, who became a Christian through his ministry. Mary may not have been as educated as her husband's new friends, but she fitted in well, as she had in Olney. In a letter, Hannah More wrote:

How could I write so much without saying a word of Mrs Newton? Only I suppose because one generally saves the best for the last. Pray tell her with my kind compliments that I regret exceedingly the inconvenient distance between us which puts it out of my power to cultivate an intimacy from which I am persuaded I should derive so much pleasure and advantage.[29]

Mary adapted to the new role of society hostess. John wrote to William Cowper, 'Often we have a succession of visitants from breakfast to bedtime.'[30]

As John's ministry grew, Mary continued to grow in her faith and to encourage and support him. John still found it easier to mention spiritual matters in letters than in person. He wrote:

My heart was melted the other day when I found the little book in your drawer, in which you had begun to set down such texts of scripture as had more particularly engaged your notice, and especially when I read the two pages of prayers with which you had prefaced them ... May He give us more freedom to converse to our mutual encouragement. Next to the salvation of my own soul, there is nothing lays so near my heart, as your spiritual welfare; and yet I am often tongue-tied, and can speak more readily to anybody than to you.[31]

Her personal trust in Christ grew through John's influence, the example of her niece Eliza and particularly during her frequent times of ill health. After her death, John wrote, 'I believe she spent ten years out of the forty that she was spared to me if all the days of her sufferings were added together in illness and pain.'[32] But she learned to trust God during these times. 'How often has He made himself known, as your Deliverer and Physician! In raising you up from the gates of the grave! May we always remember his goodness in your last affliction.'[33] John could see her faith grow stronger as her body grew weaker. 'I am persuaded that something passed then that has left a relish and effect upon your mind ever since ... Are you not determined to be His?'[34]

John always lived with the expectation of her imminent death, and was grateful to God for sparing her so many times, so that she had the opportunity to come to Christ.

O my dearest M. I bless His name for bringing us together, and for sparing us to have some knowledge, and communion, in these great things. How many that were joined about the same time with us, or since, have been separated by death! How many are living in mutual disgust! And how many who seem happy, are in reality miserable because they know nothing of the Lord and his goodness.[35]

John dreaded Mary dying before him, and wrote to Hannah More: 'When my forboding mind has anticipated the possibility of surviving my dear Mary, the question, How could I bear it? How I could ever expect to see another cheerful hour?'[36]

Eventually his fears became reality, when Mary contracted inoperable breast cancer. Her last two years were spent in agony as she disliked the effects of laudanum, the only available pain relief. John said of those years, 'My right hand was not chopped off at a stroke ... it was sawn off by slow degrees',[37] but he was comforted by her strong faith.

Whatever little contrivances we formed for her amusement in the course of the day she would attend to nothing till she had finished her stated reading of the scripture in which she employed much time and great attention. I have her Bible by me which I would not part with for half the manuscripts in the Vatican in which almost every principal text from the beginning to the end of the book is marked in the margin with a pencil by her own dear hand. The good word of God was her medicine and her food while she was able to read it.[38]

Tragically for two weeks

> *Her thoughts became clouded and confused and she gradually lost not only the comfortable evidence of her own interest in the precious truths of the Bible but she lost all hold of the truth itself. She doubted the truth of the Bible or whether truth existed. And together with this she expressed an extreme reluctance to death and could not easily bear the most distant hint of her approaching end though we were expecting it daily and hourly.[39]*

Before she died, her faith returned and she confidently looked forward to her eternal future. John adored Mary, and had relied on her presence and support. He was devastated by her death, but was determined to continue his ministry.

> *I believe it was about two or three months before her death when I was walking up and down the room offering disjointed prayers from a heart torn with distress that a thought suddenly struck me with unusual force to this effect. The promises of God must be true; surely the Lord will help me if I am willing to be helped.[40]*

Having preached so often on Christ's ability to help

those in need, he deliberately practised what he preached — and shocked some of his friends.

> *I was afraid of sitting at home and indulging myself by poring over my loss; and therefore I was seen in the street, and visited some of my serious friends the very next day. I likewise preached three times while she lay dead in the house.*[41]

He kept going, knowing that Mary was now safe with Christ. Ten years later, he wrote to Hannah More of his longing for heaven: 'There I trust my dear Mary is waiting for me, and in the Lord's own time I hope to join with her and all the redeemed in praising the Lamb, once upon the cross, now upon the throne of glory.'[42]

John's lasting tribute to his beloved Mary was the publication of his letters to her in two large volumes. Although his other works were bestsellers, the publishers were not sure who would buy something so sentimental. However, the books of letters were a great success. The mainly female readers loved John's blend of religious encouragement and devoted declarations of love. Their husbands were less keen; they compared unfavorably with the romantic John Newton.

Mary Newton was a very ordinary woman married to an extraordinary man. His love for her was a constant throughout all the changes of life. Despite not being a

Christian when they married, she never resented his faith, and humbly learned from her husband. She was never intimidated by his devotion, his intelligence or his strong character. Her care and concern enabled him to flourish and to serve. John wrote after she died:

> *She was certainly my chief temporal blessing and the providential hinge upon which all the temporal events of my life have turned. Before I was four years old she was sent into the world to be my companion and to soften the rugged path of life.*[43]

Mary was privileged to be one half of one of the most delightful Christian marriages, based on mutual faith, love and respect. After many years of marriage, John wrote: 'The blessing of the Lord upon our connection, has in the course of 35 years ripened the passion of love into a solid, and inexpressibly tender friendship, which I trust, in its most valuable properties will subsist for ever.'[44]

BIBLE STUDY
& REFLECTION

1 Corinthians 12:12–27

1. What part of the body of Christ might Mary Newton represent (v. 14)? What about you?

2. Why might Mary have been tempted to feel inferior, or that she did not belong (vv. 15,16)?

3. In Mary's life, what evidence was there that her gifts were exactly the right ones for her situation, that 'God has arranged the parts in the body, every one of them, just as he wanted them' (v. 18)?

4. In what way was weak and ordinary Mary's role 'indispensable' (v. 22)?

5. How can this encourage you, if you feel you are weak and ordinary too?

6. How can this challenge you, if you are tempted to look down on those who you consider weak and ordinary?

EPILOGUE

There you have it. Seven women from the 1700s. Some you will have loved, some — hopefully just one — you will have loathed. Each one was very different — different characters, different circumstances, different struggles. We are all different too. We may be old or young, married or single, thriving or struggling. Each one of us will have been encouraged and challenged in different ways by the women in this book, but put together there are some general lessons they can teach us, as we try to live godly lives in the twenty-first century.

First, we need to be thankful. Looking at the lives of these women should help us realize how easy our lives are today. Our homes are more comfortable than even Selina could have dreamt of with an army of servants. Our lives are longer, more healthy and, on the whole, more secure. There will be tragedies, sickness and difficulties, but rarely on a scale that was considered quite normal in the relatively recent past. Seeing how most of these women reacted to the significant hardship of their lives can help us put our own hardships in perspective. Let's be thankful for all the good things and the good times God has given us, and learn to trust in Him, as they did, when the inevitable tough times come.

Because our lives *are* generally quite comfortable, we need to learn to get our priorities straight. Sally Wesley was used to a comfortable life, and wealthy friends. She sometimes let that life, rather than the gospel, set her priorities for her family. When life is good it can be hard to keep an eternal perspective. Sarah Edwards also had a prosperous upbringing, but her focus for herself and for her family was on getting to know Christ and serving Him, rather than living an easy and socially acceptable life. Selina used her position to reach others for the gospel, but sacrificed her wealth and status for Christ's sake. In our world, with so much emphasis on material things, we need to take on the challenge to hold such things lightly and to concentrate on treasures that last for ever.

Whatever our backgrounds, we can also rejoice in our differences. Mary Newton and Selina, Countess of Huntingdon could not have been more different. Selina was confident, dynamic, healthy, independent and famous. Mary was humble, gentle, sickly and unknown. God used both of them in the situations He put them in, when they were prepared to use the gifts they had in His service. We may feel inadequate or unimportant, but God has made us the people we are and put us in a particular situation. He can use us, too, whoever and wherever we are, if we are willing to serve Him.

That means we need to be faithful. Molly Wesley and Elizabeth Whitefield both had absent husbands who put their ministry before their marriage. Both had bereavements and hard times. The key difference between them was that Elizabeth trusted God throughout and Molly did not. Molly focused on herself and her problems and became bitter and miserable. Elizabeth focused on God and his goodness, and resolved to serve Him. Whatever life has in store for us, we need to build our relationship with God now; we need to learn to trust and obey Him day by day so that we know He can be trusted in the hard times. Our instinct should be to cling to Him, not push Him away.

So ... 'since we are surrounded by such a great cloud of witnesses, let us throw off everything that hinders and the sin that so easily entangles, and let us run with perseverance the race marked out for us. Let us fix our eyes on Jesus, the author and perfecter of our faith, who for the joy set before him endured the cross, scorning its shame, and sat down at the right hand of the throne of God. Consider him who endured such opposition from sinful men, so that you will not grow weary and lose heart.'[1]

END NOTES

ACKNOWLEDGEMENTS

1. John Newton, *Letters to a Wife Written in England 1755–1785* (London: J. Johnson, 1793), p. 166.

INTRODUCTION

1. J.C. Ryle, *Christian Leaders of the Eighteenth Century* 1885 (Edinburgh: Banner of Truth Trust, 1978).
2. Hebrews 12:1.
3. Her fame lives on in the nursery rhyme 'Lucy Locket lost her pocket, Kitty Fisher found it'. Possible explanations for the meaning of this vary – Lucy Locket was a love rival; possibly the pocket was the lover or client, the source of her income; beyond that, the explanations are quite crude.

CHAPTER ONE

1. John Kirk, *Mother of the Wesleys* (Charleston, SC: BiblioBazaar LLC, 2010).
2. Charles Wallace, ed., *Susanna Wesley: The Complete Writings* (NY: OUP 1997), p. 377.
3. Ibid.
4. http://glenobrien.blogspot.co.uk/2011/08/dear-jacky-letter-from-susanna-wesley (accessed 22.3.13).
5. Adam Clark, *Memoirs of the Wesley Family* (NY: N. Bangs and T. Mason, 1824), p. 143.
6. Charles Wallace, ed., *Susanna Wesley: The Complete Writings*, p. 13.
7. John Kirk, *Mother of the Wesleys*, p.181.
8. Ibid., p.182.
9. Ibid., p. 182.
10. Ibid., p. 244.
11. Charles Wallace, ed., *Susanna Wesley: The Complete Writings*, p. 12.

12. William H. Fitchett, *Wesley and His Century* (NY: Eaton & Mains, 1908), p. 23.

13. Charles Wallace, ed., *Susanna Wesley: The Complete Writings*, p. 65.

14. Ibid., p. 69.

15. The Journal of John Wesley (Grand Rapids Christian Classics Ethereal Library http://www.ccel.org/ccel/wesley/journal.html, p. 55 (accessed 22.3.13).

16. John Wesley, *The Works of the Rev. John Wesley, .Vol 1* (NY: J. & J. Harper, 1827), p. 23.

17. John Kirk, *Mother of the Wesleys*, p. 260.

18. Ibid., p. 218.

19. Ibid., p. 232.

CHAPTER TWO

1. *The Journal of Charles Wesley*, Wesley Center Online, http://wesley.nnu.edu/charles-wesley/the-journal-of-charles-wesley-1707-1788/ (accessed 22.3.13). Excerpt reprinted with the permission of the Wesley Center Online (http://wesley.nnu.edu).

2. Aaron Hobart Crossley Seymour, *The Life and Times of Selina, Countess of Huntingdon Vol. 1* (London: William Edward Painter, 1839), p. 110.

3. John R. Tyson, ed., *Charles Wesley: A Reader* (NY: OUP, 1989), p. 318.

4. 'Hymns for Christian Friends: 16' in *Charles Wesley: A Reader* (ed. Tyson), p. 339.

5. *The Journal of Charles Wesley*, Wesley Center Online.

6. *The Journal of Charles Wesley*, Wesley Center Online.

7. *The Journal of Charles Wesley*, Wesley Center Online.

8. *The Journal of Charles Wesley*, Wesley Center Online.

9. John R. Tyson, ed., *Charles Wesley: A Reader*, p. 337.

10. *The Journal of Charles Wesley*, Wesley Centre Online.

11. J.F. Wright, L. Swormstedt, *The Ladies' Repository Vol. 27* (Methodist Episcopal Church General Conference, 1867).

12. Quoted in John Telford, *The Life of Rev. Charles Wesley, MA* (London: Wesleyan Methodist Book Room, 1900), p. 316.

13. John Tyson, *Assist Me to Proclaim: The Life and Hymns of*

Charles Wesley (Grand Rapids, MI: Eerdmans, 2007), p. 203.
14. Ibid., p. 182.
15. Ibid., p. 208.
16. *The Journal of Charles Wesley*, Wesley Center Online.
17. *The Journal of Charles Wesley*, Wesley Center Online.
18. James Thomas Lightwood, *Samuel Wesley, Musician: The Story of His Life* (London: Epworth Press, 1937), p. 14.
19. Thomas Jackson, *The Life of the Rev. Charles Wesley* (NY: G Lane & P.P. Sandford, 1842), p. 681.
20. James Thomas Lightwood, *Samuel Wesley, Musician: The Story of His Life*, p. 22.
21. John Tyson, *Assist Me to Proclaim: The Life and Hymns of Charles Wesley*, p. 209.
22. James Thomas Lightwood, *Samuel Wesley, Musician: The Story of His Life*, p. 22.
23. John Tyson, *Assist Me to Proclaim: The Life and Hymns of Charles Wesley*, p. 303.
24. Phillip Olleson, *Samuel Wesley: The Man and His Music* (Woodbridge: Boydell Press, 2003), p. 22.
25. Source unfound.
26. Thomas Jackson, *The Life of the Rev. Charles Wesley*, p. 766.
27. Wesley family documents.
28. J.F. Wright, L. Swormstedt, *The Ladies' Repository Vol. 27*.

CHAPTER THREE

1. 1 Peter 5:7.
2. Henry Moore, *The Life of the Rev. John Wesley Vol. ii* (London: John Kershaw, 1825), p. 172.
3. Doreen Moore, *Good Christians, Good Husbands?* (Fearn, Tain: Christian Focus, 2004), p. 46.
4. Charles Wesley Flint, *Charles Wesley and His Colleagues* (Washington DC: Public Affairs Press, 1957), p. 56.
5. Augustin Léger, *Wesley's Last Love* (London: J.M. Dent, 1910), p.2.
6. Augustin Léger, *Wesley's Last Love*, p. 3.
7. Ibid.
8. Henry Moore, *The Life of the Rev. John Wesley*, p. 172.

9. Kenneth J. Collins, *John Wesley: A Theological Journey* (Nashville, TN: Abingdon Press, 2003).

10. *The Journal of Charles Wesley*, Wesley Center Online.

11. *John Wesley's Letters*, March 1751, Wesley Center Online.

12. The proceedings of the Wesley Historical Society 1949–50.

13. Augustin Léger, *Wesley's Last Love*, p. 136.

14. *John Wesley's Letters*, May 1752, Wesley Center Online.

15. The proceedings of the Wesley Historical Society 1949–50.

16. Augustin Léger, *Wesley's Last Love*, p. 159.

17. Ibid., p. 161.

18. Ibid., p. 161.

19. Augustine Birrell, *Letters of John Wesley* (London: Hodder & Stoughton, 1915), p. 329.

20. Augustin Léger, *Wesley's Last Love*, p. 134.

21. H. Newton Malony, Jr *The Amazing John Wesley* (Downers Grove, IL: IVP USA, 2010), p. 130.

22. John Emory, *The Works of the Reverend John Wesley Vol. vi* (NY: J. Emory and B. Waugh, 1831), p. 728.

23. Augustine Birrell, *Letters of John Wesley*, p. 354.

24. Ibid.

25. John Hampson claimed this event took place when the Wesleys were visiting Northern Ireland. Wesley always denied the claim – perhaps because it really was untrue; perhaps because it was too humiliating to admit to.

26. Richard Watson, John Emory, *The Life of the Rev. John Wesley* (NY: J. Emory and B. Waugh, 1831), p.189.

27. John Emory, *The Works of the Rev. John Wesley Vol. iii* (Philadelphia, PA: D. & S. Neal & W.S. Stockton, 1826), p. 356.

28. Luke Tyerman, *The Life and Times of the Rev. John Wesley MA Vol. ii* (London: Hodder & Stoughton, 1870), p. 112.

29. Augustine Birrell, *Letters of John Wesley*, p. 356.

30. *John Wesley's Letters*, 1751, Wesley Center Online.

31. Henry Moore, *The Life of the Rev. John Wesley*, p. 176: 'He has repeatedly told me that he believed the Lord overruled this whole painful business for his good and that if Mrs Wesley had been a better wife and had continued to act in that way in which she knew well how to act he might have been unfaithful in the great work to which the Lord had called him and might have too much sought to please her according to her own views.'

CHAPTER FOUR

1. Stephen Tomkins, *John Wesley: A Biography* (Oxford: Lion Books, 2003).
2. William Jay, *Memoirs of the Life and Character of the Late Cornelius Winter* (Philadelphia, PA: B. Redman, 1823), p. 62.
3. Joseph Beaumont Wakeley, *The Prince of Pulpit Orators: A Portraiture of Rev. George Whitefield, M.A.* (NY: Carlton and Lanahan, 1871), p. 278 .
4. John Pollock, *George Whitefield and the Great Awakening* (Oxford: Lion, 1986), p. 140.
5. John Pollock, *George Whitefield and the Great Awakening*, p. 142.
6. Luke Tyerman, *The Life of the Rev. George Whitefield*, http:// quintapress.macmate.me/PDF_Books/Whitefield/Tyerman_ volume_1_v1.pdf, p. 551 (accessed 22.3.13).
7. Luke Tyerman, *The Life of the Rev. George Whitefield Vol. i*, p. 551.
8. Luke Tyerman, *The Life of the Rev. George Whitefield Vol. i*, p. 551.
9. John Richard Andrews, *George Whitefield: A Light Rising in Obscurity* (Boston: Adamant Media Corporation, 2002).
10. Luke Tyerman, *The Life of the Rev. George Whitefield Vol. i*, p. 626.
11. Robert Philip, *The Life and Times of the Reverend George Whitefield, MA* (London: George Virtue, 1838), p. 263.
12. Luke Tyerman, *The Life of the Rev. George Whitefield*, http:// quintapress.macmate.me/PDF_Books/Whitefield/Tyerman_ volume_2_v1.pdf, p. 86 (accessed 22.3.13).
13. Ibid., p. 89.
14. Ibid., p. 148.
15. Ibid., p. 146.
16. Robert Philip, *The Life and Times of the Reverend George Whitefield, MA,*(p. 268.
17. Luke Tyerman, *The Life of the Rev. George Whitefield Vol. ii*, p. 148.
18. Robert Philip, *The Life and Times of the Reverend George Whitefield, MA*, p. 358.
19. Luke Tyerman , *The Life of the Rev. George Whitefield Vol. ii*, p. 211.

20. George Whitefield, *The Journals of George Whitefield* (Oswestry: Quinta Press, 2009), p. 705.

21. *A Select Collection of Letters of the Late Reverend George Whitefield Vol. 3* (Edinburgh: Edward and Charles Dilly, 1772), p. 68.

22. Ibid., p.71.

23. Ibid., p. 260.

24. Luke Tyerman, *The Life of the Rev. George Whitefield Vol. ii*, p. 485.

25. Ibid., p. 306.

26. Thomas Jackson, ed.,*Charles Wesley's Journals Vol. 2* (London: John Mason, 1849), p. 235.

27. Luke Tyerman, *The Life of the Rev. George Whitefield Vol. ii*, p. 317.

28. *A Select Collection of Letters of the Late Reverend George Whitefield Vol. 3*, p. 372.

29. Ibid., p. 373.

30. *A Select Collection of Letters of the Late Reverend George Whitefield Vol. 3*, p. 373.

31. Ibid., p. 382.

CHAPTER FIVE

1. Sarah's grandson, Aaron Burr was the third US vice-president under Thomas Jefferson. In 1804 he was accused of murdering a political rival in a duel. A few years later he was accused of treason, having attempted to raise an army to create an independent state in the south-west of North America, which he intended to rule himself.

2. A.E. Winship, *Jukes–Edwards: A Study in Education and Heredity* (Harrisburg, PA: R.L. Myers & Co., 1900).

3. Jonathan Edwards, 'Sarah Pierrepont', in *Jonathan Edwards: Basic Writings* (ed. Ola Elizabeth Winslow; NY: The New American Library, 1966), pp. 66,67.

4. Jonathan Edwards, Henry Rogers, Sereno Edwards Dwight *The Works of Jonathan Edwards Vol 1* (NY: G. & C. & H. Carvill, 1830), p. 106.

5. The inventory also included a patch box in which to keep beauty spots.

6. Sereno Edwards Dwight, *Life of President Edwards* (NY: G. &

C. & H. Carvill, 1830), p. 129.

7. Iain H. Murray, *Jonathan Edwards: A New Biography* (Edinburgh: Banner of Truth Trust, 1987), p. 313

8. Sereno Edwards Dwight, *Life of President Edwards*, p. 127.

9. Ibid., p. 1113.

10. Ibid., p. 127.

11. Ibid., p. 129.

12. Ibid., p. 131.

13. Ibid., p. 435.

14. Ibid., p. 436.

15. Ibid., p. 436.

16. Ibid., p. 437.

17. Ibid., p. 437.

18. This is reproduced in full in Dorothy Z. Baker, Sue Lane McCulley, ed., *The Silent and Soft Communion: The Conversion Narratives of Sarah Pierpont* (Tennessee, TN: University of Tennessee Press, 2005).

19. Interestingly he did not give her name, or even say she was a woman, but referred to her only as 'the person'.

20. *The Works of President Edwards Vol. 3* (NY: Leavitt & Allen, 1857), p. 305.

21. Jonathan Edwards, Henry Rogers, Sereno Edwards Dwight *The Works of Jonathan Edwards*, p 285.

22. George Marsden, *Jonathan Edwards: A Life* (New Haven, CT and London: Yale University, 2003), p. 302.

23. The letter can be found in full in Iain H. Murray, *Jonathan Edwards: A New Biography*, pp. 485–7.

24. Jerusha Edwards died at the age of 18, having cared for the dying missionary David Brainerd.

25. Sereno Edwards Dwight, *Life of President Edwards*, p. 440.

26. Sereno Edwards Dwight, *Life of President Edwards*, p. 486.

27. Dorothy Z. Baker, Sue Lane McCulley, ed., *The Silent and Soft Communion: The Conversion Narratives of Sarah Pierpont*, p. xx.

28. Sereno Edwards Dwight, *Life of President Edwards*, p. 442.

29. Sereno Edwards Dwight, *Life of President Edwards*, p. 580.

30. Sereno Edwards Dwight, *Life of President Edwards*, p. 580.

31. All Stephen J. Stein, ed., *The Cambridge Companion to Jonathan Edwards* (Cambridge: Cambridge University Press, 2006), p. 48.

32. Iain H. Murray, *Jonathan Edwards: A New Biography*, p. 441.
33. Proverbs 31:28–30.

CHAPTER SIX

1. Margaret later married Ingham – an earl's sister marrying a Methodist preacher must have been quite shocking.
2. Aaron Hobart Crossley Seymour, *The Life and Times of Selina, Countess of Huntingdon Vol. 1*, p. 14.
3. Ibid., p. 50.
4. Sarah Tytler, *The Countess of Huntingdon and Her Circle* (London: Sir I. Pitman & Sons, 1907), p. 80.
5. Ibid., p. 80.
6. Helen Knight, *Lady Huntingdon and Her Friends* (American Tract Society New York 1853), p. 36.
7. Ibid., p. 40.
8. Aaron Hobart Crossley Seymour, *The Life and Times of Selina, Countess of Huntingdon Vol. 1*, p. 85.
9. Helen Knight, *Lady Huntingdon and Her Friends*, p. 63.
10. Ibid., p. 74.
11. Ibid., p. 75.
12. Rev. Thomas W. Aveling, *Memorials of the Clayton family: with unpublished correspondence of the Countess of Huntingdon Lady Glenorchy; the Revs John Newton, A. Toplady etc. etc.* (London: Jackson, Walford & Hodder, 1867), p. 16.
13. Calvinism placed more emphasis on God's action in salvation, Arminianism more on people's.
14. Mudge Zachariah Atwell, *Lady Huntingdon Portrayed* (NY: Carlton & Porter, 1857), p. 177.
15. Aaron Hobart Crossley Seymour, *The Life and Times of Selina, Countess of Huntingdon Vol. 2*, p. 478.
16. Aaron Hobart Crossley Seymour, *The Life and Times of Selina, Countess of Huntingdon Vol. 2*, p. 282.
17. Whitefield left the Bethesda Orphan House to Selina in his will. She never visited and controversially tried to make it financially viable by increasing the number of slaves. It eventually burned down, and the American Revolution meant that it was never reopened.
18. Rev. Thomas W. Aveling, *Memorials of the Clayton family with*

unpublished correspondence of the Countess of Huntingdon ..., p. 161.

19. Lydia Howard Sigourney, *Examples from the eighteenth and nineteenth centuries* (NY: Charles Scribner, 1857), p. 56.

20. Aaron Hobart Crossley Seymour, *The Life and Times of Selina, Countess of Huntingdon Vol. 2*, p. 480.

21. Aaron Hobart Crossley Seymour, *The Life and Times of Selina, Countess of Huntingdon Vol 1*, p. 464.

22. Rev. Alfred H. New, *Memoir of Selina Countess of Huntingdon* (NY: Protestant Episcopal Society for the Promotion of Evangelical Knowledge, 1858), p. 421.

23. Helen Knight, *Lady Huntingdon and Her Friends*, p. 279.

24. Mudge Zachariah Atwell, *Lady Huntingdon Portrayed*, p. 303.

25. Aaron Hobart Crossley Seymour, *The Life and Times of Selina, Countess of Huntingdon Vol. 2*, p. 502.

26. Aaron Hobart Crossley Seymour, *The Life and Times of Selina, Countess of Huntingdon Vol. 2*, p. 499.

27. Christopher Ness, *An Antidote Against Arminianism* (London: J. Bennett, 1836), p. 35

28. Newman Reader, 'Essays Critical and Historical', *British Critic* October 1840.

CHAPTER SEVEN

1. Jonathan Aitken, *John Newton: From Disgrace to Amazing Grace* (Wheaton, IL: Crossway Books, 2007).

2. John Newton, Bruce Hindmarsh *The Life and Spirituality of John Newton: An Authentic Narrative* (Vancouver, BC: Regent College Publishing, 1998), p. 31.

3. Ibid., p. 32.

4. Ibid., p. 33.

5. Ibid., p. 64.

6. Ibid., p. 92.

7. John Newton, *Letters to a Wife Written During Three Voyages to Africa 1750 to 1754* (London: J. Johnson, 1793), p. 119.

8. Jonathan Aitken, *John Newton: From Disgrace to Amazing Grace.*

9. Jonathan Aitken, *John Newton: From Disgrace to Amazing Grace.*

10. John Newton, *Letters to a Wife Written During Three Voyages to Africa 1750 to 1754*, p. 118.

11. Ibid., p.149.

12. Josiah Bull, *But Now I See: The Life of John Newton* http:// shatteringdenial.com/books/autobiography_of_john_ newton_but_now_i_see.pdf (accessed 22.3.13), p. 34.

13. John Newton, *Letters to a Wife Written During Three Voyages to Africa 1750 to 1754*, p. 147.

14. John Newton, *The Works of the Rev. John Newton Vol. 1* (London: Published by the direction of his executors, 1808), p. 87.

15. John Newton, *Letters to a Wife Written During Three Voyages to Africa 1750 to 1754*, p 23.

16. John Newton, *Letters to a Wife Written in England 1755– 1785* (London: J. Johnson, 1793), p. 31.

17. Ibid., p. 34.

18. Ibid., p. 25.

19. Ibid., p. 55.

20. Ibid., p. 74.

21. Ibid., p. 74.

22. Ibid., p. 166.

23. Ibid., p. 180.

24. Jonathan Aitken, *John Newton: From Disgrace to Amazing Grace.*

25. John Newton, *The Works of the Rev. John Newton Vol. 6*, p. 586.

26. Recreational sea swimming was unheard of for women at the time, but getting into the sea was believed to have health benefits.

27. John Newton, *Memoirs of the Rev. John Newton ... With selections from his correspondence* (London: Seeley and Burnside, 1838), p. 214.

28. John Newton, *Letters to a Wife Written in England, from 1755 to 1785* p. 231.

29. John Newton, *Memoirs of the Rev. John Newton ... With selections from his correspondence* (London: R.B. Seeley and W. Burnside London, 1843), p. 220.

30. Jonathan Aitken, *John Newton: From Disgrace to Amazing Grace.*

31. John Newton, *Letters to a Wife Written in England, from 1755 to 1785* p. 114.

32. John Newton, *Memoirs of the Rev. John Newton ... With selections from his correspondence*, p. 231.

33. John Newton, *Letters to a Wife Written in England, from 1755 to 1785* p. 106.

34. John Newton, *Letters to a Wife Written in England, from 1755 to 1785* p. 111.

35. John Newton, *Letters to a Wife Written in England, from 1755 to 1785* p. 109.

36. Josiah Bull, *Letters of John Newton of Olney and St Mary Woolnoth* (London: The Religious Tract Society, date unknown), p.311.

37. Josiah Bull, *Letters of John Newton of Olney and St Mary Woolnoth*, p. 311.

38. John Newton, *Memoirs of the Rev. John Newton ... With selections from his correspondence*, p. 234.

39. John Newton, *Memoirs of the Rev. John Newton ... With selections from his correspondence*, p. 234.

40. John Newton, *Memoirs of the Rev. John Newton ... With selections from his correspondence*, p. 234.

41. John Newton, *Memoirs of the Rev. John Newton ... With selections from his correspondence*, p. 234.

42. Josiah Bull, *Letters of John Newton of Olney and St Mary Woolnoth*, p. 358.

43. Josiah Bull, *Letters of John Newton of Olney and St Mary Woolnoth*, p. 358.

44. John Newton, *Letters to a Wife Written in England, from 1755 to 1785* p. 221.

EPILOGUE

1.   Hebrews 12:1–3 (NIV, 1984).W

10Publishing is the publishing house of 10ofThose.
It is committed to producing quality Christian
resources that are biblical and accessible.

www.10ofthose.com is our online retail arm selling
thousands of quality books at discounted prices.
We also service many church bookstalls
and can help your church to set up a bookstall.
Single and bulk purchases welcome.

For information contact: sales@10ofthose.com
or check out our website: www.10ofthose.com